TALES OF THE ATLANTIC PIRATES

by Geoffrey Girard

First edition

1 2 3 4 5   09 08 07 06 05

Cover and interior illustrations by Brian Rappa.
Cover and interior designed by Desiree Rappa.

For the Captains and Firstmates of
the Cavalier, Dandee, Intensity, and Island Girl

Who long ago taught me my port from my starboard and
introduced me to the magical world of sailing.

ACKNOWLEDGEMENTS

Special thanks to Mr. John Buettner at Washington College for instant information and support. To Mr. Marshall Cramer at the Country Folk store in historic Smithville, for suggesting 1920's rum runners would make a good story backdrop if I ever wrote a book about pirates. To Mr. Harry Leeds for his continued encouragement and spirit. To Ms. Kathy Brock for her keen eye and editorial assistance. Thank you to Kathy Poulton, librarian extraordinaire of Moeller High School, who deftly supplied research materials and a quiet place to write. To Blake Koen at Middle Atlantic Press for always keeping things sailing forward.

Specific research thanks to The Friends of the *Hunley*, the National Underwater and Marine Agency, and the Middletown Township Historical Society. *Life Among the Pirates* by David Cordingly and *A History of Pirates* by Nigel Cawthorne proved the flagships of this book's extensive research and I recommend both as a fine start for your further reading.

To friends and family who supported the process throughout.

CONTENTS

O'ER the glad waters of the dark blue sea,
Our thoughts as boundless, and our souls as free
Far as the breeze can bear, the billows foam,
Survey our empire, and behold our home!
— *The Corsair,* Lord Byron

INTRODUCTION

While writing this book, pirates made the news after attacking a luxury cruise liner just off the coast of Somalia. Yes, *pirates*. Firing machine guns and a grenade launcher, these modern-day Blackbeards attempted to board the cruise ship from several small speedboats, but were ultimately held back and outraced by the bigger ship. Their interest was money, their means was violence. And though the catch proved too big that morning, they escaped easily to try again another day. Closer to home, piracy has been recently reported off the coasts of Haiti and Jamaica.

The tales you're about to read are based on the actual history and legends of the many pirates who once sailed along and terrorized America's lengthy Atlantic coast. Movies and literature typically portray such men as adventurous rogues, colorful and exciting. While you'll also get plenty of that in this book, make no mistake about it: Golden Age pirates were close mates of the gang who stormed after that cruise ship. They were violent men who lived outside society's rules. And though that's always been interesting to the rest of us, there's a good reason pirates of old were eventually hunted down and wiped out by civilized men.

Pirates openly sailed our eastern shores from 1600 to 1800, and somewhere between that history and the legends that followed lies the half-truth of their adventures and legacy. And that, perhaps, is just the way any respectable pirate would want it.

CLOSE TO THE WIND

1671, NEW YORK

"Ye want to be a pirate, do ye?"

"Yes."

"What be your name then, laddie?"

"Gallagher, sir. Tomas Gallagher."

"Sir, is it?" The dark-skinned man cackled coarsely and his gang snickered behind him. "Very proper this one 'e is, mates! Ye look familiar, 'Proper Tom.' Seen ye before, 'aven't I?"

"I don't know."

"Our capt'n ain't lookin' to recruit no sad cases, understand. What can ye bloody do?"

"Cook. Clean."

"Whale's bile! If we needed that, I'd 'ave brought me own bloody mother aboard." The men laughed again. "Tie me a double overhand." He tossed a short rope across the table. The crowded Gravesend tavern, a sweltering room that stank of stale sweat and beer, brimmed with bodies and noise. Atop the nearest table, one of the dockside girls whirled about as the other men cheered and tossed coins at her feet. The knot was returned, checked, then tossed aside. "Perfectly wretched. What a skinny maggot, ye are, too! No good with a blade either, I imagine."

"Not yet."

The pirate chuckled, took another swig of ale. "E'er sailed the 'igh seas?"

7

"No."

"Men die out thar."

"I understand."

"*You'll* likely die out thar, Proper Tom."

"Could use an honest cook, Clemmy," One of the others spoke up. "E'en if only for a few weeks. Ain't had a fittin' meal since Bloody George got kilt."

The first pirate tugged the wide golden hoop at his ear, thinking. "Would be agreeable to 'ave a proper cook again, I suppose. Though, you'll curse your own mother for birthin' ye. We'll work ye to the bone, listen. Here's yer articles." He shoved a sheet of paper across the table. "Says you get 'alf a share to all plunder 'ereto. Compensation of six 'undred pieces for a lost arm, one 'undred if ye lose an eye —"

"I can read."

"Can ye, laddie? Then read the rest, ye maggot, and sign away your pitiful soul at the bottom."

The contract was signed and pushed back.

"Well then, ya lil' wharf rat, welcome to the crew of the *Rambler*. I 'ope you're now quite prepared to meet Captain MacLaren, the most terrible rogue this side of 'ell."

"I am," she said.

☠ ☠ ☠

Naturally, Emily found the only other woman on board, and even though the paint in her rosy cheeks had faded, and there were tiny nicks along her neckline, Emily had come to believe she was possibly the most beautiful thing in the whole world. After all, the *Rambler* was home to seventy-four men — seventy-four filthy, crude, riotous men — and it was rather nice to see another girl every now and again. Even one made of wood.

Emily Pieper, known to her immediate world as "Proper Tom" for more than two weeks now thanks to a vile haircut and a tight bandage wound around her chest, lay peacefully in the lower netting just beside the

8

ship's bowsprit. The Atlantic rolled and swished beneath her, the *Rambler's* bow cutting though its cool dark waters. Above, the stars gleamed like floating diamonds in the pitch-black sky, and the lines sang and slapped in the warm wind. Between her booted feet, she could still watch the men gathered on deck around the lanterns. Drinking again, and laughing, engaged in some stupid game with a sack of rats they'd caught below. Biggens played at his fiddle, occasionally mumbling a bawdy verse in accompaniment. Emily quietly hummed along too, a familiar tune already, and turned to look at her only companion.

The wood carving of the ship's figurehead was slightly larger than lifesize, the woman's body backed against the stemhead at the top of the bow and wearing, via the intricate woodwork, a beautiful crimson dress with faded golden trim at the shortened sleeves and low-cut neckline. Long straight black hair ran below her shoulders. Her skin, revealed at her throat and graceful arms and hands, was golden and healthy, her right arm crossed just beneath her rounded bosom. Her left hand, graceful and elegant, held the drapery of her skirt. Her face was lovely, sharp featured with a small nose and full lips that would have appeared somehow too sensual if not for her large, intelligent eyes. Painted the color of the whole world, all blues, greens, and browns. They'd been carved to show intensity and interest. Finally, around her neck hung an oval pendant, a single smooth ebony stone.

"The men have determined," she told the figure in a whisper two sisters with a secret might use, "that tomorrow at dawn, we will attack the Dutch ships."

The wooden face did not respond, of course, but Emily didn't mind. Just having someone to talk at was enough.

More so than any physical dangers she'd predicted, a pirate's ship had proven a lonely adventure for a young girl in disguise. To help protect her secret, she'd kept away from the others whenever possible and, since she prepared a fine stew and accepted her other various duties without complaint or direction, the men seemed just fine with that arrangement. Even her necessities had been easier to manage than she'd thought they'd be, once she'd learned the men's patterns and timetables.

It hadn't been easy at first. They'd watched her carefully and made things quite difficult indeed. She'd been kicked, her head smacked more than once for easy laughter, tripped while serving dinner, spit on and farted at, and awakened with buckets of cold sea water. Her first night, she'd even been challenged to a knife duel and declined courteously amid their teasing laughter, fleeing the lowers to cry in private at the ship's bow. That's when she'd found the wooden woman. And for two weeks, each night, she'd managed to cry only in front of her.

After their first boarding and the sea storm just off Connecticut, when her oft-predicted *'orrible death* had not actually happened — and to her amusement, more than one bet had been paid off on that matter — the men relaxed and she'd simply become one of them. It was that simple. Only Duncan still glared at her with hate now. Duncan, with his single cruel blue eye and heavy black boots. She winced at even the sound of those boots, and though he had not yet kicked her, she knew she would be sore for days when he finally did.

"Perhaps they will need me to board tomorrow," she'd brought her hands behind her head and closed her eyes to the night. "Wouldn't that be something?"

"Lights out, mates," Captain MacLaren's voice suddenly cut over the men's festivities. "The dawn will come quick enough and we've work to do when it does."

Emily moved her foot to get a better look. He stood tall at the quarterdeck in a grey shirt and his blue-trimmed vest, a cutlass and crimson waist sash slung over his black pants. His greying hair hung free, several braids curled along the side of his strong whiskered chin. The captain's dark eyes raked the deck as the men scattered quietly to their bunks. She watched as he assessed the lookouts posted at stern and masts, then spoke briefly with the helmsmen on call. He looked at her suddenly, the dark eyes locked on her own over the toe of her boot. He briefly shook his head, then moved back to his own cabin.

Captain Tully MacLaren. A villainous pirate.

Her father.

A man she hadn't even met until she'd taken the name Proper Tom and joined a band of death-courting pirates just two weeks before. And here she was, the daughter he'd forgotten at birth, the family he'd left behind for dead some fourteen years before when her mother died in childbirth.

And soon, she had resolved, *I might even tell him so.*

Emily turned, smiling tiredly at the wooden woman. "Good night," she whispered.

☠ ☠ ☠

The Dutch merchant ships sailed from Bayonne likely laden with treasure and voyage supplies. Two yachts, small two-masted vessels with ten-man crews and one swivel gun per ship, were the pirate ship's prey.

The *Rambler* leapt from the morning fog like a kitchen cat onto a sleeping pair of mice, and the two foreign ships split, one racing east deeper into the Atlantic the other back towards the coast of New York. "We're weathering on 'er, me 'earties," the captain shouted over the pirates' cheers. "We'll have at 'er soon enough! North-west now!"

"Aye, Captain!" The pirate ship, black flag waving high in the morning wind, veered for the second vessel, bearing in on its shoreward course. Emily watched the chase from the safety of the quarterdeck, where she'd helped to hand out guns with Luesch, the lanky Weapons Master. The ships pulled closer.

"Duncan! Clemmy! Admiral Bone!" Captain MacLaren roared the names over the wind in the sails, the slapping rigging, and the excited men along the railings. "Board her quick and make short work of it. Meet ye right quick just off Great Kills."

"Aye, sir," replied three pirates in unison.

"Duncan, why don't ye take Proper Tom along for good measure."

What??!! Emily froze. Stole a glance at the dreadful pirate at her side. Saw his missing eye, the dark empty socket, scarred and pink, staring back. She stepped slowly backwards.

"Aye, sir." Duncan's good eye now glared at her for an instant, freezing her in place, before turning back to his own team at the gangplanks. The eye had looked pleased.

She'd been given as good as a direct order during combat. Vanishing now would mean certain death. The first Dutch ship was in striking range and several of the *Rambler's* cannons suddenly exploded. The shots passed over the Dutch bow and hails for its surrender followed.

"Avast!" the captain, her father, hailed the Dutch. "Avast ye distant dogs or we'll kill the lot of ya with a bloody broadside."

The vessel slowed, and the two ships drew together while the ocean's waves lapped and splashed between them. Duncan stepped suddenly in front of her and Emily's nose came only to his tattooed and sweaty chest. "Whatever good it will do ye," he snarled and shoved a short cutlass into her hands. The blade felt cold and heavy. "Stay close to the others, and do what you're bloody told or I'll gut ye meself, ye scrawny bilge rat. Ye know, even better than I, that ye don't belong here."

The Dutch ship came about, wind spilling from its sails. The *Rambler* pulled along side, the railing pulled away while the prize crew crowded at the gangplanks.

Biggens, the fiddler, appeared beside her. "Ain't nothing to worry about, laddie. They're outnumbered four to one and 'ave no good reason to fight. Just other people's money to them." His eyes gleamed with excitement and, she suspected, beer. He carried two muskets in his belt and a wide boarding axe in his hand. "Might not even 'ave to kill that many of 'em."

Dark shadows swung above her, as boarding ropes spun through the air, and men leaped from the *Rambler's* ratlines to the Dutch ship. The three teams the captain had selected jumped between the two ships as screams filled the morning, piratical shouts of triumph and warning. Emily fell in with the others, but, at the ship's edge, gripping the cutlass, she stopped. The ocean sloshed beneath her, the boats shifting on the ocean's current, the gap between the two vessels sliding back and forth from a mere foot to four in a single moment. The Dutch boat rode higher, also. Water splashed over her legs and jeers and curses of "Gangway!" gathered behind her. Another moment, she thought. The waves brought the two boats closer again, *close enough*, and she jumped for the Dutch ship.

Her boots slipped on the Dutch gangway, and she fell, both hands grabbing for the railing. But her reach was short, the wrapping under her arms too constricting. Her knee exploded in pain as the cutlass tumbled off the hull into the ocean. Water raced across her back.

She was slipping into the sea.

An arm grabbed her own, strong and pinching, and lifted her onto the Dutch ship. It was Biggens.

"First jump's always a curse," he grinned. "Gets easier, laddie. Meet ye at the quarterdeck."

Emily straightened herself, gingerly touching the deep cut at her knee. The *Rambler* had already shoved off, moving out to sea for the second ship. She could still hear her father's voice, though: the captain again giving directions to his crew over the sea's winds.

Up top, the Dutch had apparently surrendered without a fight. She wandered in amazement along the gangplank as the crew moved about the ship, systematically stripping it of everything of value, loading it forward for the predetermined assembly point and the *Rambler's* eventual return. She found eight men tied to the jib mast. The last, the ship's skipper, lay over the closed hatchway, pinned back by several pirates.

She saw that Duncan himself leaned over the prisoner, forcing what looked like two long fuses between the man's fingers. "I'll ask ye again, mate," she heard him say.

Emily stood shaking, rooted in her spot, when the fuses were finally lit. The Dutchman began screaming in a language she'd never heard before, but she wondered if she'd even recognize it in his shrieks if she had. Duncan and the others only laughed. Emily found that she'd pushed slowly forward, forcing her way into the scene.

"Won't tell us where the treasure's hid," Duncan turned his cold blue eye at her. "'Tis a matter of sound judgment, it is." The man's fingers were turning black, peeling away, the sparks leaping off his flesh.

"Please," she said suddenly. The sound was lost beneath the man's rising screams. Once more she tried, more to the prisoner than Duncan. "Please."

"Ahoy, men! It's Proper Tom to the rescue," Duncan laughed, lifting out his arms. "And bloody right, 'e is, too. I never once said 'please' to the daft bugger." The other men roared as one in laughter. Duncan leaned into the captive, his face just inches away. "Now, won't ye please tell us where the treasure's hid?"

Later, aboard the *Rambler*, as the crew drank in celebration and carefully catalogued the plunder from the two ships, Emily retreated again to the bow. And to her only friend.

The men had burned the two ships for attempting to flee, and the Dutch merchants, a crew from Gorkum, were collected and freed on a single launch. Duncan reduced her small share by half for the lost cutlass. Emily didn't care. She'd never wanted the money. But, staring over the bow, as the ship cut through the shadowed waves of a full moon, she now wasn't sure what she wanted at all. When she'd run away from home, from her Uncle Randolph and his wife, it had seemed so simple. *Find your father.* Over the years, she'd finally wrested his name from her guardians, some of his most scandalous exploits, and even his gang's known lairs. The rest had been easy enough. But now...

She looked back towards the others where he, the captain, stood amidst the men, laughing hoarsely and pointing enthusiastically out to the far black sea.

Emily sat down at the bow, knees crossed, and looked at the wooden women. The moonlight gleamed along the figure's dress and the side of her smooth face. "Just wait until you hear about what happened today," she said.

Emily lay in the bow's netting again, resting after a long morning of scrubbing out the galley. The shadow of the wooden woman beside her covered the girl's face from the afternoon sun as she absently gazed at the wooden face and mused over the past weeks. She'd been a pirate for a little more than a month now. They'd taken several more ships after the Dutch vessels, with good loot taken from each. Some of the men were already pushing hard to head back to shore for a spell before the long trip South. Over the course of events, she'd been taught to properly double load the cannons and to tie a rolling hitch. To drink lemon juice to fend off the scurvy. She'd even earned some navigational sense and to move about the ratlines some, climbing with an ease and agility many of the larger men struggled with.

"She's beautiful, isn't she?"

Emily jerked, found her father standing at the bow above her. "Captain! I — Sorry, sir, I..."

He held out his hand to stay her struggles in the netting. "Easy," he said. "Easy now, there. Proper Tom, is it?"

"Yes, sir."

He smiled again under his shaggy beard. "Enjoying your time with us?"

Emily shrugged, looked away from his stare. She'd struggled up to a sitting position.

"I notice ye spend a bit o' time up 'ere. Ye found 'er after all."

"Sorry, sir. I never meant — Her," she stopped. "Yes, she is a beautiful carving."

"'Er name is Rosaline," he said.

Emily shuddered. It was her mother's name.

"Commissioned the piece ten years ago now. Only me memory to go on then. Paid a pretty coin, too, as ye might imagine. But worth it. Aye? Beautiful, as ye can see. And, a fine women too, by God. Stronger and sassier than 'alf the men on this ship, she was," he scratched his beard in memory. "A terrible dancer, though, I recall."

Emily tried not to smile. "Where — How did you know her?"

He pointed towards the coast. "Met 'er in Bushwick, I did. Was running with Captain Flecknoe's boys, and we'd put in for the winter. Met her then. Fell in love as young folk be apt to. Caused quite the scandal, too, naturally. With 'er family. The rest is... Well."

"What happened?" Emily's voice trembled when she spoke and she hoped he hadn't heard it.

"There was talk of settling down. Dear Rosaline doin' most of the talkin', naturally," he grinned. "But, it sounded right enough. She made it sound so. And we was properly married, ye might say. And —"

"A baby!" she blurted.

His eyebrows rose. "Indeed, Proper Tom. A wee whisp born one April eve. An angel in starlight, 'er mother said. Emily, she became. Born with a full head of hair, but small as a fairy's child. Was even there meself. Alas, poor Rosaline did not survive the night."

She found she'd turned to study the wooden face. Both weathered and magnificent. The face of the mother she'd never known. "I'm sorry," Emily said.

He shrugged. "This is the way of the world, yes."

My mother.

She looked back at the pirate captain where he remained gazing over the portside, staring bleakly towards the shore.

"I was twenty, with little but the strength in me arms to offer her," he said. "And Rosaline 'ad a brother, praise be. A proper man, a good man with a family of 'is own and a civilized job. For a baby girl. Told me they'd take 'er on so long as they ne'er saw my contemptible soul again." He chuckled rough and short. "Well, civilized men, you know."

Emily nodded and a single tear escaped to run down her dirty face. She wanted then to leap from the netting and throw herself into his arms. To tell him everything.

She resisted the impulse.

"Quite the prize tonight," he said, clearing his own throat. "The *Triumpherant*, ye know."

"Yes." The British warship they'd been tracking for days. Half its crew was now believed on leave in Brooke Land. "Ten cannons aside. Won't it be dangerous?"

16

"Aye. It's what we sometimes call *sailing close to the wind*," he said. "A deed dangerous, or perhaps, even, a wee bit stupid, for the chance of a greater, grander prize."

"I see." She'd looked down from his seemingly judging gaze.

"So, for instance, in this case," he added, "Those cannons will prove a fine addition to our battery."

"Yes, they will. Captain MacLaren, I —" She looked back up. "I wanted to —"

"We'll speak again after," he stopped her. Smiled awkwardly. "Besides, swabbie, shouldn't you be below preparing dinner?"

She nodded.

"Well then." He stepped away as quickly as he'd first appeared. Emily waited until he'd vanished into the bustle of the other men and then set for the galley herself. To make dinner for herself, her father, and seventy-three other pirates.

Five launches set out at midnight, the oarlocks oiled and the paddles wrapped and muffled for stealth. The gig carried twenty men, the four jolly boats ten. In all, sixty pirates rowed towards the British warship *Triumpherant* to catch its reduced crew by surprise and then courteously free the King's ship from the heavy burden of her cannons. Emily, left behind on the *Rambler* with a small ghost crew, now watched the various wakes of their small crafts fade into the darkness.

She moved slowly towards the bow, hoping for some quiet time with Rosaline before the men came back. Halfway, she spotted Duncan and her whole stomach clenched. Of all the nasty rats to be stranded with. The cruel one-eyed pirate must have read her very thoughts, because he suddenly looked at her, then vanished into the lowers with two other sailors. "Maggot," she cursed after him, then looked down at the figurehead. "He's an absolute maggot," she said again, liking the sound of it from her own mouth.

The top of the figurehead, Rosaline's long dark hair, gleamed against the moonlight. Emily restudied the careful carving, already knew every lock and curl by heart. Each crease in the back of the dress. She wondered if the dress had been real or simply part of the Captain's imagination. And, if it had been real, what dances had it, *she*, seen? What dinners?

Emily suddenly found herself thinking how the others were faring. The crew. How far from the British warship. "A man-of-war," she said aloud. "Can you imagine?"

She noticed the other men then. A group of four gathered beneath the main mast. They spoke aggressively, but she could not hear what they were saying. Something was happening. That much was sure, and Biggens, the fiddler, was among them.

She looked out over the ocean now towards where the boats had rowed. "What do you suppose we'll say when he gets back?" she asked suddenly. "What could we possibly talk about?" She picked at the railing, thinking. "And do I even *want* to talk to him? Do I?"

Before the wooden figure could answer, not that Emily expected it ever would, everything exploded. She crouched down instinctively, her stomach leaping to her wrapped chest, her shoulders balled in fear. A single cannon blast, she realized. One of the twenty pounders it sounded. Its clamor filled the whole night, every corner, then echoed across the entire Atlantic to England herself. Emily's heart now beat like a loose sail in a windstorm. Had the *Triumpherant* attacked?

It had not. The blast had come from the *Rambler* itself.

Even now, the smoke lifted from the smoldering gun and one of the men moved away from the cannon as others swept to the masts. Who were they shooting at? Echoed shouts rolled back from afar. Gunshots rang out in the darkness far beyond.

Emily moved forward. The *Rambler's* foremast had gone up now and two men were struggling with the mizzenmast too. They were planning to move somewhere, and quickly. She moved towards the main mast. "Biggens," she called out as the pirate pushed past in the opposite direction. "Biggens. What happened? Why —"

"Stow it, boy," he snapped, his eyes darting and wild. "Or you'll be serving breakfast for Davy Jones tomorrow." He continued on his way, rushing to the quarterdeck. She heard angry shouts from the poop deck, and then a musket shot. Emily stood rooted beneath the mainmast. Now, she finally understood.

It was a mutiny. A full blown mutiny. No doubt led by the faithless beast Duncan. These men had fired the cannon intentionally. To rouse the British, to warn them. To give up the other men. To betray her father. Now, surely the warship had stirred awake. And, even with a smaller crew, it was still a warship with a full compliment of guns.

The five open boats were doomed. They'd be picked from the water by the Brits as easy as snatching driftwood. Then, most — including the father she'd only first spoken to minutes before — would end up at the wrong end of a rope, dancing with Jack Ketch. It was too horrid, too terrible. It was — it was, she resolved, unacceptable.

If she could get below and find a pistol, or — the ship was already moving. West, away from the shore and the purposely abandoned men. If she could only get the boat turned around.

Cannon fire exploded in the distance, echoing. The warship had finally let free its own cannons in the night.

The armaments below, she thought suddenly. The cutting-out crews had likely taken most, but there was still a chance that a few pieces had been left behind. Emily raced for the hatchway of the lower decks. Down the steps, she again found the lowers as cold and dark as any imagined grave. She'd never cared for the lower decks. They'd always been stale and damp, creepy, and stinking of body odor and spoiling food. Rats typically scurried about in the shadows, ran over the barrels and beams just inches from her face. No matter. She moved through the darkness towards the armory.

Above, she heard the sound of bootsteps stomping, moving frantically across the top deck. Six, maybe ten men struggling to set the sails where thirty would usually be on hand for the same job. *Ten men*, she groaned. *Even with a weapon, how shall I dare hope to stop even one?*

She found the gate locked, several pistols including a blunderbuss, which made any marksmanship unnecessary, still inside. She scrambled for something to break the steel padlock. Among the bunks, Emily found a rusted dagger sticking horizontally from one of the quarter beams. Likely tossed into the rafter years before as part of some stupid boy game. She grabbed the dirty hilt with both hands and tugged. The blade held. "Hell!" she grunted and put one boot against the beam for extra leverage. She pulled again, slowly working the dagger free.

Now in her possession, she turned the blade and used the head of its hilt to knock against the padlock. She slammed several times, the padlock swinging in its catch. *Too loud*, she thought. *They'll hear me.* She looked for something to muffle the next strike. Wrapped the hilt with an old bit of shirt. Smashed it down again. Nothing. Struck once more. The blade cut into her hand. Again she tried.

The padlock popped. Swung about, the shackle fallen loose and open. Emily tucked the knife away and patted her fingers together before her face, clapping. *I did it, I did it.* She threw off the padlock and opened the gate.

The hand that grabbed her from behind was strong and enormous. It wrapped her mouth and chin, clenching the whole bottom half of her face. Her scream vanished in the meaty paws as the fingers dug painfully into her skin. The hand was clammy and stunk of bilge water and grease.

Her mouth still covered, a second hand grabbed her by the back of her shirt, also pinning the blade there, and slowly turned her around. She saw the boots first and her next scream was lost in his hold.

Duncan.

"It's Proper Tom to the rescue," he whispered in the darkness, leaning into her. The voice was almost playful, his haggard face scrunched tight and angry. His breath was fast and heavy. There was blood on his cheeks, and the empty socket of his missing eye glared at her like the black eye of Death. His single eye burned into her own wide-eyed stare.

Traitor, she raged beneath his hold. He'd betrayed all of them. It was as she'd always suspected from such a villain. He looked back into the blackness behind them, the passage leading away. "Some of our mates have chased a bad idea," he said quietly.

She thought furiously, loosened some against his hold, and Duncan slowly lifted his hand from her mouth. Her own breath was loud and fast in the cramped quiet passage.

"Good," he said.

"Are you — "

"Hush, Proper Tom. We don't have the time."

"I thought — I saw you with them."

"Ramos and Tackett lured me below with some fiction 'bout the well," he replied. "Tried to drown me like a rat in the same." He smiled. "Alas, ye won't be seeing Ramos or Tackett again."

He'd stepped into the armory and began fitting himself with several pistols and a cutlass. "There are still six," he said, breathing heavily. "Only six. But I can not," he said, loading a pistol, "solve the misfortune of their vile existence while also turnin' the ship round to fetch the others." He primed the pistol and handed it to her. "Ye be the one who must bring the ship back to the others. Savvy?"

"Yes," she found herself saying.

"North by Nor'west. No more than 'alf a league now. Follow the sounds of shots and shoutin'. Our mates will be fightin' for their very lives, Proper Tom." He took a half sword from the racks and added it to his waistband. "Get to the quarterdeck. I'll get back to ye as soon as I be able. Can ye do it? Good, then." He had not waited for her reply, but pushed past her and vanished again into the shadows of the lower decks as quickly and quietly as he'd appeared.

Pistol shots rang out above.

Emily bolted forward, tucking the rusted dagger and pistol into her own belt. The hatchway loomed ahead and she scurried up its steps, testing the weight of the pistol Duncan had given her. She heard cursing, and the sound of more musket fire. Two men dashed over the gangplanks directly past her. Moving towards the bow, away from the quarterdeck. Duncan luring them away.

Emily crept from the cover of the hatchway onto the decks. The night's air was cool and fresh after the lowers, full of promise. She darted along the gangway, the quarterdeck just ahead. Up the steps, she found they'd tied off the wheel. A crew of six would have to. Her new dagger made easy work of the line.

Taking the wheel in her trembling hands, she looked to the sails. The mutineers had managed to set the fore topgallant and topsail, the mizzen topsail and the main course. It was enough. Would be more, even, once she turned about into the wind back towards the others. Emily checked the compass. North by northwest.

The ship looked so big, the whole *Rambler* stretched out before her.

Emily turned the wheel sharply, pulling it hard to the right, the spokes crossing beneath her hands. The ship healed wildly against the sudden turn as the sails and spars snapped round, the wind spilling away into the night. It creaked and shuddered as water and wind rushed across the vessel, sloshing and fluttering. The yards moaned as the braces swung around. Lines and shrouding snapped. Mizzen sails beat. Another series of pistol shots rang out on the forward decks. A hundred sounds filled her ears as the sloop turned at last on her new line. Several sails flapped futilely, desperately in need of trimming, but the wind caught in enough and the ship suddenly lurched forward.

On the forward decks, she could make out several dark shapes dancing about the moonlight and the sounds of cutlasses clashing together drifted towards her. One shape made for the gangway, dashing back towards the quarterdeck. Towards her.

Emily fumbled for the pistol, keeping one hand on the wheel. Keeping the hundred-ton ship straight against the sea. The same shape fell suddenly, a single scream lifting on the wind. Still, the ship pressed forward.

In the dark ocean ahead, she could hear guns being fired and men shouting. The shadow of something black and enormous loomed on the dark horizon. The *Triumpherant*. The British warship now emerged in the darkness. Tiny sparks of gunfire sprang from its large decks.

Ahead now, she could see the smaller boats in the black water. The swarming men inside fired back at the British warship, the larger vessel pressing onto them, gunfire falling upon the trapped pirates like black hail. One launch already lay smashed to pieces, tossing in the ocean. She could not see them yet, but Emily knew men were dead or dying in those same rolling waves.

The *Triumpherant* turned towards the ship, her ship. Changing tack to pull along beside her. Its cannons glistened in the moonlight. She counted twelve on the side. The pirates in the smaller boats between shouted and waved for her to stop, to help, to do something. Anything. She looked far ahead towards the bow, and the figure of Rosaline, again leading the ship. If only she could ask her what to do. If only she could talk to someone...

Moments from being blasted to scraps, Emily sensed another danger even closer at hand. Biggens, standing at the steps of the quarterdeck. He carried a cutlass and his eyes, even in the dark, shined with hate.

Emily immediately lifted and fired her pistol. The sound was almost lost in the rushing wind and the harried shouts of men on all sides of her. Its acrid smoke stung her eyes.

But when the cloud lifted, Biggens had only moved closer up the steps. And he was smiling.

She thought of the dagger at her hip. Dropped the spent pistol, drew it free. She knew it would not be enough against the pirate's long cutlass. It would —

Something pounced atop Biggens then. There were screams. Duncan. It was Duncan. The two pirates crashed over the quarterdeck's railing to the deck. Swords rang out.

She looked again at the British warship. The white-uniformed men aboard shouting, no doubt preparing to give the *Rambler* the full broadside of twelve cannons. If she could only cut the warship. Cut it in half. Emily looked to Rosaline again, to the carving of her long-lost mother. She thought of the bow. The sharp, angled bow. Almost like a sword, she realized suddenly.

The wheel turned in her hands. The ship shifted again, turning directly towards the *Triumpherant*. *There would be no broadside now*, she thought. *I have narrowed the target.* The ship pressed forward. Bearing in on the warship.

She would ram them. Cut the Brits in half if need be. Rosaline would protect them. Emily knew that she would. The pirate ship turned more, running directly at the center of the enemy vessel.

Cannons fired. A thunderous roar followed immediately by exploding timbers and snapping spars. Sails split and whistled. Men shouted in the darkness between. She pulled the wheel again, pulling off enough, and the two ships collided, the *Rambler's* massive bowsprit shattered in an eruption of sound and movement.

The bowsprit snapped, the ship's prow now slammed into the British ship's lower front hull. The whole *Rambler* roared, timbers ripping and the front sails collapsing on themselves in a spray of line and clatter. Water splashed over the bow of the ship and the whole vessel shuddered with the impact. Emily found she'd been knocked to the deck, and fought to pull herself back to the wheel.

When she had, Duncan now stood at her side. He took the wheel and turned the ship portside, away from the trembling warship.

"Just away from their short guns," he said. "The mates are already moving to the chains. I'll need your help to drop some extra netting for them. We have three minutes before they fire again."

"Yeah," she said. She felt tired suddenly and somewhat dazed.

"What about the —"

"Don't worry 'bout them, no more, Proper Tom."

"And Biggens? Is he —"

"Him?" Duncan smiled. "Aye, I asked him to stop breathin'." He reached out to tousle the top of her head. "And I even said *please.*"

He winked his lone eye and Emily had no choice but to smile.

☠ ☠ ☠

The ship's figurehead. The wood carving was splintered into thirds, the wood fractured and frayed, the long fragment of what was once a beautiful crimson dress jutting from the stemhead. The collision had destroyed the head, torn another hole through the stern. Emily could just make out the bottom of her black hair and the start of her right arm. But there was no necklace anymore, no rosy cheeks and rounded lips. No eyes the color of the world or golden skin. Only splintered wood, exposed and grey.

She'd helped save fifty-three men the night before, and in doing that, lost the only person on the ship she'd ever really known or cared for. Her only reprieve was that she was too tired to cry.

"Our hero," a voice said behind her.

She remained still, looking at the destroyed figurehead.

"Expected to find ye here."

She turned to him slowly.

"Took quite the toll on me boat, ye did."

"Yes, sir."

"And on me Rosaline, too, I see."

"Yes."

The captain studied her for a moment. His eyes were sharp and serious. "Well, in consideration of the full matter, I 'ereby release ye of any further consequence."

"But Rosaline! She was your —" She gasped. "How can you ever —"

"'Ush, child," He drew the cutlass from his hip and it sang silver in the ocean's wind. It gleamed in the rising sun. "There be far greater tributes to a woman's beauty, to 'er life and spirit, than some costly wood carving."

He held up the sword, turning it towards her, and, in its wide curved blade, Emily now saw her own reflection. And understood.

The straight black hair and olive skin, her face sharp featured with a small nose, full lips and large, expressive eyes painted the color of the whole world, all blues, greens and browns.

MacLaren pulled the blade back slowly, resheathed it while Emily turned to look over the Atlantic towards the tree-lined New York coast. "We'll be puttin' in at Gravesend in a few days," he said. "Before we 'ead to the West Indies for the winter."

"I understand."

25

He scratched at his ear some. "Unless, of course," he muttered, "Ye was plannin' to stay aboard aways?"

She turned to him. "I was, in fact."

"That so?"

"If you approve, of course?"

The pirate nodded. "Fine, then. Approve? Yes, yes. Of course, I — It — It will be pleasant to 'ave someone to talk to, won't it?"

"Yes."

"Well then," he said, "It's been a long night, swabbie. I'd best be gettin' some rest."

She nodded.

"Good night then, Emily," he said.

"Good night, Captain."

NOTES: *Female pirates were rare, but certainly not unheard of. Men often sneaked wives and sweethearts aboard disguised as men, or, women themselves chose to pursue the profit and freedom typically not offered elsewhere in colonial society. Dozens of women ultimately became successful and infamous pirate captains, including several along the Atlantic coast: Sarah Bishop (a native New Yorker turned privateer during the Revolutionary War), Flora Burn (during the 1740s) and Virginian Mary Crichett. While Crichett was ultimately hung for her crimes, complete leniency was typically shown to women pirates as courts usually executed the men and released the women outright.*

Chinese and Egyptian sailors likely began the ritual of painting oculi(eyes) on the bows of their vessels, believing the decoration enabled the ships to better find their way. The Phoenicians, Greeks, and Romans embraced the custom in turn and the prow adornments grew increasingly more complicated over time to include the carved likenesses of gods, mythological creatures, and family members. The figureheads remain forever linked to the superstition that these images were guardians of the vessels and sailors firmly believed that their wood icons were endowed with magical powers.

SHADOW ISLAND

1685, NORTH CAROLINA

The island was silent and lifeless.

Only the waves moved along its empty shore, and their soft swish and grumble broke again and again over the dark sand. Gabel sat just beyond their reach and watched the far grey horizon. Still waiting. Still hoping. But less so each time.

How long had it been? Sixteen days, twenty. Maybe only four, he mused. It was hard to tell anymore. For awhile, time had become one meaningless blur.

Now, he sat along the shoreline, another night watching the indifferent Atlantic. No craft spotted yet again, as he'd been assured there wouldn't be. His thoughts naturally turned to Marwood.

It was Captain Marwood, after all, who'd condemned Gabel to his current fate. Marwood, who'd somehow managed to sniff out their mutinous scheme and then enforced his characteristic justice. Swift and spiteful. Under Marwood's *management*, men were routinely flogged with the cat-o'-nine, or tied to the mast without food or water, or, even keelhauled when he'd felt particularly affronted. But for Gabel, Marwood had chosen something else, something special.

After all, Gabel hadn't just overslept and skipped a night watch or gotten too drunk before a boarding. His crime had been outright treason. Mutiny. For the Royal Navy or even a merchant's ship, those accused were punished with death. Aboard a pirate vessel, the penalty was often worse.

John Hitch, Gabel's co-conspirator, had already been hauled away to some dreadful end. What form of unspeakable torture he'd been made to endure before that end, Gabel had no idea. Nor did he want to. Even now, he cringed, simply thinking of the doomed look in his friend's eyes, the sheer glee in Marwood's, as the other men led the "traitor" below deck. The Captain knew a thing or two about pain, in all its diverse and innumerable forms.

Gabel looked up and down the desolate beach. His punishment. To be marooned. Abandoned on a barren island somewhere off the Carolinas. Where true pirates often died suddenly in battle on crowded decks, he'd been left to die slowly and alone.

It was not unheard of. He knew stories of other sailors doomed to similar fates. It was the pirate way. But sailing under Marwood's flag, he'd actually never seen it done. Until now.

The Captain had even gone so far as to sail once around the entire island to let Gabel see the whole of his new home. A prison, more likely his tomb. No more than a few miles wide, split in half by a small jungle of dark trees in the center and jagged rock croppings along the north and south shoreline. He'd been left with only the clothes on his back. And the pistol.

For as a final token of mercy, or scorn, Marwood had tossed him a flintlock pistol with a single round. A means to a swift end for when Gabel had enough. It was well known that men often went mad when marooned in such desolate places without any other human contact, no water but the rain, and little hope for rescue.

Madness? Sometimes, Gabel hoped that's all that it was. That he'd simply gone insane. Somehow, that would be easier to accept than the other.

The ginger flush of dawn now traced the edge of the horizon and Gabel rose to move back to his cave. He had to.

The sun would be rising soon.

And with it, the shadows.

Gabel crouched against the jagged wall and tried not to watch the narrow opening. He knew the sunlight now flushed its top. In the cave's darkness, he gnawed at the gull's claw and found some slivers of salty gristle on the thin bone. It had been three days since he'd killed the bird and he'd now had the last of it. He felt exhausted, but couldn't sleep.

He'd heard strange sounds again just hours before, the same weird cry now that moved over the island on the ocean's warm breeze. A ghostly wailing heard many nights and days before, inhuman yet somehow...

In the dark, Gabel's fingers nervously tapped the flintlock pistol at his side. It still held the single shot Marwood had left him, promising protection or immediate escape. He fought again to keep his thoughts from the second option as his eyes moved uneasily about the rim of the cave.

He'd found it as shelter, a place to escape from the sea's winds and rain. It had become his fortress. He closed his eyes in the cave's darkness and wondered again at the madness that had driven him here.

He pictured Captain Marwood standing at the stern of the small landing craft. His gaunt form had swayed easily with the wave's current, his dark hair stirred oily and wild in the sea winds behind his ears. A worn leather tricorn hat with a single feather sat upon his head, and his skin was brown as the hat, cracked from years at sea, and dark patches dotted his face and arms. But it was the eyes that Gabel thought most of now.

He'd struggled to look away from that never-ending stare during the short passage ashore. Assumed he'd find fierce hate in his captain's eyes, but saw something else there. To Gabel, it looked a little like amusement.

When they landed on the shore, the other men waited in the craft while Marwood led Gabel up the beach alone. Gabel walked ahead, moving forward, waiting from some indication as to what he was supposed to do. The Captain hadn't spoken a word to him in hours, and the silence between them now was like the silence of a crypt.

For several steps, Gabel expected to simply be executed. The Captain, as usual, was certainly armed for the dirty task. In his wide crimson-red sash, he'd carried a slender cutlass and two pistols. This was not, alas, the Captain's intention.

Instead, Marwood stopped walking and then casually plopped down in the tan sand. He'd patted for Gabel to join him, and when he saw that Gabel would not, shrugged and went ahead. "Tell ye a tale," he said. His voice was low and rough. "'bout an island."

Gabel stood a few feet away and watched as Marwood looked over the beach back towards the infinite Atlantic. The waiting *Theodosia*, his only home for almost two years, hovered at anchor just before the horizon. Beyond that, there was only more ocean.

"A 'undred years ago," Marwood said, "Savages be using this 'ere land. And I don't be meaning the wild Squantum or Powche. The 'eathens who canoed out to this cursed place be shunned and feared by such tribes. These redskins worshipped far darker gods. 'Eld to customs most unnatural, most foul."

Gabel eyed the cutlass stuffed in the Captain's belt and wondered for just a moment if he were fast enough to snatch it away.

"'Uman sacrifices," Marwood continued, "Bloody affairs. Unspeakable. And, in one final ceremony, or so the yarn goes, the entire tribe be butchered. Every man, every woman and every child sacrificed to some abominable faith."

Gabel waited. The strange ways and cruelty of some of the tribes were well known. He'd heard such tales before and anticipated his captain's aim. *He wants to scare me.*

"For years, they called the island 'aunted. Sailors warned that spirits of the tribe still be walkin' its dark shore and dead forest. Men 'ear unusual sounds." Marwood turned to face him. "And they be seein' things. *Strange* things."

"Is that so?" Gabel replied absently.

"In the shadows," the pirate said, half smiling. His teeth were crooked and half-rotted black. "That's wot they said. The lost tribe's ghosts. Banshees. Whatever ye be callin' such an objectionable thing. Sailors are said to 'ave vanished, and ships kept away for years. Until Ingemar."

Gabel had not heard the story before, but recognized the name of the infamous pirate. Captain Ingemar. A sadistic predator who'd mostly sailed the

African coast, he recalled. Also perhaps, that Ingemar had once been some kind of warlock, a practitioner of the dark arts. Not an all together uncommon trait among the more notorious pirate captains.

His own captain, who likely drank tea with the very devil himself, had turned his gaze back to the sea. "Ingemar and 'is crew be along the Atlantic that spring and needin' a private spot for careenin'. They'd 'eard the stories, of course, but, well, their cap'n insisted."

Marwood chose a small whelk shell from the sand and dusted it off with his breath. Gabel waited for him to speak, half-turned to study the dim tree line behind them.

"Just one," the captain toyed with the shell between his knotted dark fingers. "One survivor. Only lasted a few days 'imself. Insane, don't ye know. But before 'e'd passed, 'e spoke some about what'd happened. Peculiar stories. All 'bout bleedin' altars and mounds of bone. Said the very shadows gotten into 'is cap'n somehow. That Ingemar 'ad gone ravin' mad. That they'd all been — There'd been some *unpleasantness*."

Gabel knew the kind of "unpleasantness" Marwood spoke of. It was one of the fiend's favorite euphemisms.

"This, in and of itself, weren't that bizarre," the Captain said. "Many a sailor gone mad at sea. Or, while stranded for a wee bit ashore. Something to do with the sun, perhaps, or maybe just the terrible isolation. But, in this 'ere matter, the man also claimed that something still moved o'er the island. That 'e'd seen, well, that 'e'd seen their shadows. In the trees, along the beach."

"Bilge slop," Gabel cursed. *It was nonsense.*

"Undoubtedly," Marwood smiled again and tossed the shell back towards the ocean. "As for Ingemar, no one knows for sure. Some say 'e, too, still be walkin' the island. Possessed. A cursed spirit quite eager, don't ye see, for company."

The Captain stood slowly and pulled one of the flintlock pistols from his belt. He tossed it to Gabel. "Take it," he said. The gun's handle was worn smooth with use.

Gabel wondered briefly if it were already loaded. Marwood dropped a small leather bag on the sand between them. Gabel knew, by pirate's tradition, that it was likely one lead ball and some gun powder. "'Ow you use it is up to you," the Captain smiled and started back to the other men.

Gabel calculated how long it would take him to get the pouch open and load the pistol. He figured he might have one shot at Marwood before he made it to the boat. Instead, he just watched as his former captain returned, without another word, to the dinghy, and the men rowed back to the *Theodosia*. Within an hour, the ship had disappeared beyond the horizon.

He turned to examine his new home. His first thoughts were of finding shelter and fresh water. He'd need food too. As for the rest, he'd assumed Marwood was only teasing, a final taunt as Gabel was left to his grim fate. Then, just a few days later, he saw it all for himself.

☠ ☠ ☠

It had been less than a week when, moving knee deep in the spurting surf, hunting stingrays along the shore, he noticed the second shadow. Where his own shadow moved along the wet sand beside him, stretched up the beach by the morning sun, he now saw another.

Just caught it out of the corner of his eye, moving beside his own. Another dark shape. The definite figure of another man's shadow standing just behind him.

Gabel whirled about.

There was, of course, no one there. The beach remained wholly empty.

The pirate turned the other way and still nothing. His eyes followed only his own shadow, watched its distorted shape stretch back towards the small forest away from the shoreline. He wondered what trick of light he'd just seen. Some ripple in the waves, perhaps.

It's too hot, he thought suddenly, and immediately felt the cruel sun on his back.

Seeing things already, he'd laughed at himself. He supposed it was inevitable. He'd sung the few songs he knew and carried on one-sided conversations with the small crabs he'd found for breakfast. Anything to keep his imagination from putting "shadow men" in his mind. Gabel didn't give it

32

another thought until a few days later when he saw them again. At the altar of bones.

He'd discovered it while gathering wood for the night's fire. The trees were far too small for a canoe and he'd found nothing to use to rope together an escape raft. But, he could still have fire. He could enjoy its heat, its light, a reminder of civilization. In the trees, though, Gabel found another souvenir of man. Of what men, he would not make himself imagine.

The altar was black marble, chiseled from a single stone into a perfect circle that emerged four feet from the ground. It looked as if it grew directly from the center of the island itself. As if it had always been there. How else to explain its being there? The slab was perfectly smooth and polished and almost aberrant in its exactness. The sun streaked across its surface, and the absolute blackness shone like a dark jewel. None of the island's foliage had grown over it, he noticed, or even up to its gleaming base. In fact, the only thing around the platform were the skulls.

Dozens of human skulls, hundreds even, in a variety of sizes and hue, were stacked neatly along the sides of the altar. Others lay in five small piles around it. Many appeared clearly weather-worn and ancient. Others looked as if they'd only been beneath the sun and rain a few seasons.

Gabel suddenly felt nauseous looking at it all and turned away. He thought of Captain Marwood and his tales of sacrifice, of the strange natives who'd once wandered the island's forlorn shores. What ghastly men had so devotedly prepared these bones? And for what dark sacraments?

He carefully lifted one of the skulls from the pile and studied the dark sockets, considering what poor soul might have once occupied the discolored bone. He noticed the rotted clothing then, an old blue jacket he thought, and a rusted cutlass lost in the weeds. More bone peered at him from the decay.

A shadow passed suddenly over the skull in his hand, a dark shape that bent over the rounded bone and moved up his arm. Gabel dropped the skull as if he'd been bitten and the pile at his feet clattered apart into distinct skulls. One of the bleached heads even rolled across the toe of his boot.

He noticed now that other shadows played between the thin sun-streaked trees. They swayed between the branches and shifted across the dark trunks. On all sides, it seemed, he was surrounded. His mind put shapes to them, human shapes. Again, he told himself, a trick of the light.

Gabel felt chilled suddenly. He felt fear.

Though he'd certainly experienced the sensation before, whether leaping over brawling gangplanks with a cutlass in each hand, or racing up the ratlines in full gale storms, this was something else. This fear clawed slowly up his back, sharp nails pricking at his skin, and settled around his neck. He felt as if he were literally being choked by it.

He screamed in the unnatural silence, and the strangled sound echoed through the shadowed trees which seemed to jump about more excitedly. Gabel reached for the flintlock pistol at his belt and fumbled to cock it.

A dark shape, a human form he thought, now shifted over the black dais. It was not his own shadow.

He saw what looked like arms and hands reaching towards him through the trees.

Gabel had run, and the shadows followed as horrific screams burst from the forest behind him.

☠ ☠ ☠

One night, just before dawn, he spotted the ship.

The faintest hint of a dark profile on the horizon and small lights, the lanterns of the night watch, flicked within its shape. For a long time, Gabel didn't move. He wondered if the ship was even really there. When he finally stood, it was clumsily. It had been days since he'd eaten, probably days since he'd slept. He staggered towards the ocean.

"Here," he cried weakly. His voice was rasping and frail. It was a sound he hadn't heard in more than a week. "I'm here," he tried again. Another sound he didn't recognize.

Gabel waved his arms and tried shouting more. The attempt was pathetic. He was just too tired, and the ship moved slowly along the coast, passing him by.

The lustrous hint of morning now emerged slowly behind it. In a few minutes, the ship would be gone forever. His thoughts became frantic. He needed a fire, something they might notice. He needed wood. But, he'd not been back within the trees since that day at the altar. The trees simply held too many dark corners and shade that shifted with the moving sun. It was too *dangerous*.

He trailed along the shore beside the vanishing ship and his mumblings carried his internal debate. Even if he could get the wood, there wouldn't be time to start a fire. It was already too late. No need to go into the trees, after all.

Miraculously, though, the ship turned, bore windward south of the island, perhaps heading for the western shore. It was a second chance. If he could only get to the other side.

Gabel looked again at the trees. Through them was surely the clearest path to the opposite beach, and it was still dark enough. There would be no shadows. The cloud-streaked moon above did not have enough light and the tinge of dawn draped over the black ocean, waiting.

He touched the gun lodged at his belt, found some comfort there, then moved away from the beach. The trees waited just above, and their tall lean trunks stretched into the night like bunches of colossal coffin nails. Each cluster was swathed in utter blackness as the pirate stepped bravely over the edge of the tree line.

It was dark, and the gaunt branches blocked any light as Gabel began his race through the trees. They swept by as black shapes, dead and uncaring. He stumbled past each and his labored breath filled the few spaces between. The foliage at his feet grew denser and more jagged, and the roots and bushes slashed at his legs. He felt so tired. *How long has it been*, he thought, *since I've truly slept?*

An unnatural wail echoed suddenly over the island. He could no longer deny the sinister truth that he was not alone on the island. That something had likely seen the approaching vessel too, and just maybe it was something that also knew he'd risked venturing into the trees again.

Gabel raced forward, his hands pushing away branches as he stumbled through the dense wood. The dawn broke and its golden hue crept up the beach behind him. Its dim glow mixed now with the moon's fish-scaled glimmer. Now, the dark outlines all looked the same. Suddenly, Gabel felt turned around. He felt lost. The trees all looked exactly the same. He turned clumsily and his feet tripped over a fallen branch.

He cursed and crashed, exhausted, to the ground. At once, the shadows fell across his prone body and their dark streaks rolled from the trees across his legs. There were so many.

He grunted at them like some animal and scrambled back to his feet. His eyes scoured frantically above the trees, found the approaching sunlight and moved west towards the ship. He felt as if he'd already crossed the island twice, and he couldn't figure out where he'd gotten turned around.

Gabel cursed again in frustration. He no longer cared if the woods were "haunted" or "unlucky" or filled with the walking shadows of the dead. He only wanted to reach that ship.

He sprinted more furiously now. Another hundred feet, he thought, another hundred. He'd run so far already. Suddenly there was a path he recognized, and he raced towards it. Then Gabel skidded into the clearing and tried not to spill over again. He'd been right. It was a path he knew. He'd been here once before.

The circular altar sat in the middle of the clearing. Its unnatural blackness almost illuminated the surrounding dusk, and something dark and wet trickled over its edges and down the sides. It looked just like blood. He could hear it running along the wall and spattering over the stacked skulls beneath.

Gabel stood frozen. It made no sense. He was caught half awake in the strange nightmare that now played out before his eyes. His legs trembled. He thought again of the men who'd lived on the island years before. The dark rituals they'd performed. Sounds now crackled in the woods around him, and he turned following the noise. Dawn crept through the wood and the trees now bled shadows in every direction. His eyes raced over the confused shapes and shades.

Gabel stopped turning. His scream was choked and quiet.

Between the trees, just beyond the altar, he could see the distinct outline of a man.

It was cut in black, and the wide stance and silhouette of cornrowed hair suggested a seafaring man. Gabel's mind struggled with the possibility. The other ship could not have launched a landing crew yet. There was no one else on the island.

The outline of a pistol emerged from the dark shape. Gabel fell backwards away from the altar. "Leave me be," the figure snarled. Its voice was scratchy and sorrowful. The voice of some terrible dead thing.

Gabel stumbled away backwards and now considered the only other possibility.

The cursed ghost of Captain Ingemar.

Just as Marwood had warned, the horrid pirate's ghost still walked the island, looking for more sacrifices.

The shadow spoke again. The voice was broken and ghastly, and the words were mumbled and threatening.

Gabel fumbled with the pistol at his belt.

"Leave me be," he yelled back at the shade. More forms twisted and flickered between the shadows. They surged towards him.

Gabel drew the pistol. Clicked back the hammer.

The black shape now filled the entire opening behind the altar, the sun creeping round the trees towards it. Gabel eyed the twisted shadow of the pirate's ghost and lifted his gun.

He saw the gleam of its black eyes. The darkness there reminded him perfectly of the dreadful altar. "Be gone, Devil," he cried, his hand shaking. He wondered if a single musket ball could stop such a spirit.

"What be ye?" the thing demanded in a hissing voice. Then it, too, lifted something.

Gabel fired his pistol.

There was an explosion of sound and a flash of light as the thing fell back behind the black altar. Smoke filled the small clearing and the gun had dropped from Gabel's hand.

He stood trembling in the shadows for some time, afraid to see what had actually happened. What was now behind the altar?

Then he felt the wet warmth at his belly.

His hands moved down, felt it hot and oily. His fingers were now blacker in the strained light. He collapsed to one knee.

He crawled slowly forward towards the altar. Kept his own eyes on the watching skulls as he passed. His stomach ached now. He felt the bullet there and saw the red of his blood under the day's new sun.

When he finally reached the other side of the altar, the other body there was twisted awkwardly and still.

He saw the man's boots, the weathered pants of a sailor. Gabel took in the flintlock pistol laying beside the still form. He was sure he'd seen that before somewhere, too. As he crawled closer, the clearing somehow grew darker despite the mounting sun. He dragged closer.

The dead man had changed, of course. His beard was thicker than Gabel remembered, and he looked gaunt and tired. Weeks stranded on a desert island could do that to a man. Gabel knew this. And Gabel's one bullet had stuck the man squarely, killing him instantly.

John Hitch, Gabel's co-conspirator. The man who'd been hauled away to some dreadful end. Left on a desert island, it now seemed, with only a pistol and a single shot. Stranded on a haunted land, a terrible isle inhabited only by another pirate's ghost.

Gabel fell beside him and finally closed his eyes to ultimate shadow.

Except for the waves in the distance, the island was silent and lifeless.

NOTES: *While everyday reprimand came to pirates in the form of whippings or being tied to the mast for a few days without food or water, serious offenses were often punishable by torture and death. The pirates had learned such brutal ways under previous* employment, as most seafaring crews, from merchant sailors to naval marines, routinely emphasized the same system of harsh command and penalty. After all, the dangers of the open sea demanded it. There's little historical evidence of pirates actually making anyone "walk the plank," but the practice of abandoning disloyal crewmen on deserted islands was quite popular. Accounts hold that the condemned man was traditionally left with a gun and a single bullet. Shadow Island is based on the dozens of small islands off the coast of North Carolina, many of which are believed haunted to this day.

CONTEMPT OF COURT

1701, NEW JERSEY

The pirates arrived in March. Not all at once, but in a slow trickle that flooded as the trial grew closer.

They came on foot and by boat, and two even arrived along the King's Highway aboard a stylish carriage. Several were old men, dark-skinned and furrowed by years beneath the sun and tattooed in faded inks. Another was no more than eleven, simply tattooed. A few stayed at the Lincroft Inn wearing fashionable garments and jewel-topped rings, as others lurked about the town's two taverns with dirty blouses and dirtier faces. As many as twenty by the end of things. Or fifty, or three, depending on who would later tell the story. For years, Gillian Graham swore to any who'd listen that there'd been more than a hundred in the courtroom that day.

Middletown, nestled along the shores of Raritan Bay, was not unacquainted with such men, having seen its share of all forms of seamen over the years. Fishermen, merchant sailors, British navy, retired privateers. All quite similar when compared against merchants and craftsmen. Browned, hard-bitten at the eyes and hands by the wind and sea. Heavily whiskered and grubby with a fondness for ale, lascivious company, and brawling. So, unless the man in question strolled down the cobble-stoned lanes with several pistols hanging from his belt, only the most observant eye could tell the difference between a shore-leaved merchant seamen and a shore-leaved pirate. That same observant eye would have seen it in the walk, maybe. A certain swing in the shoulders, a swagger that suggested a different breed of man all together.

41

Moses Butterworth was such a man, and even though he entered the courtroom shackled at the hands and ankles and escorted by two bailiffs, he maintained that unique confidence in his manner and short steps. He wore a long black jacket with a stylish white cravat, dark blue knickers, and striped socks that ended in buckled leather shoes. He'd pulled his greyed hair back in a short ponytail, his peppered beard was trim and neat around his thin lips. His sharp face appeared relaxed, bored even, as if the event were merely a nuisance, an unnecessary distraction from a good nap or, perhaps, a nice lunch with one of the local lasses. He looked to be in his thirties with a weathered face, or a man of sixty with a boyish face. Either way, his eyes burned bright and green with life as he was marched past the assembled crowd.

The Proprietor's Governor himself had come all the way from Burlington to administer over the trial. Andrew Hamilton, a Scotsman by birth, sat atop the judge's stand, glaring over the room in his long dark robes and corkscrew white-powdered wig. He looked anxious, his typically sharp-featured and somewhat distinguished face turned frail, wan, and a bit skeletal in the lamplight. And with good reason.

The Proprietors of the colony, and their staff, weren't particularly popular with the fine citizens of New Jersey of late. For that matter, neither were the Royal Governor or his administration. Whether it was the financial owners of the colony or Queen Anne herself, the people of New Jersey didn't differentiate much. They usually hated them both. And where other colonies complained with letters to England and voiced outrage at church gatherings, the "Jarzies" were better known for showing their municipal frustrations through total riot or the occasional clubbing of random politicians.

Hamilton looked over the crowd again, his tension evident in the tightness of his grip on the polished mahogany judge's bench. The townspeople had crammed all the rows below and were now parading into the upper hall. Their noise proved a low, deep murmur that filled the whole courthouse like a swarm of giant bees. To Hamilton's left waited the local court clerk and the state's Attorney General, who would prosecute the controversial case. Two additional justices had come from Camden to render the trial's verdict. None of the five men had ever set foot in Middletown before so they had no way of realizing the growing mob was also filled with a fair number of souls who'd also never been to the town before that day. Things might have gone differently for all of them if they had.

"We will bring these proceedings to bear," Hamilton said at last and banged at the podium with his gavel twice, then waited for the crowd to settle in. "The citizens of New Jersey hereby — "

"This is an outrage!" someone in the crowd shouted from the start.

Hamilton's face creased in validation, he'd expected no less, his mouth half open as if to speak. Equally startled, but a good deal more amused, the accused, Butterworth, turned in his chair to get a better look at the commotion behind him and found a middle-aged man dressed in a merchant's stockings and coat marching down the center aisle towards them. "You've no right to hold this court, Gov'nor," the man shouted at Hamilton. "The Proprietors have no authority to bring this man to trial."

Hamilton drew himself up. It was the objection he'd feared, the protest he'd expected. "You, yourself, sir," he snapped, his own voice cold with forced civility, "shall be arrested if ye do not desist from this disturbance. Who are you, sir?"

"Samuel Willit, *sir*. Of Middletown." The merchant marched forward to stand just behind Butterworth. The two bailiffs half moved in to stop him, but Willit held up a hand to stay their approach. "And, by law and practice, any crime that may have been committed by this man at sea is to be judged by the Admiralty Court in England." He skewered Hamilton with a baleful glare. "And, that's a far cry from Burlington, sir." Cries of "here, here" filled the hall and Hamilton gaveled them away.

"The *Royal* Governor —" Hamilton emphasized *royal* to make sure everyone in the room understood the difference between his own appointment by the Proprietors versus that of his counterpart, a Governor chosen by the very Queen of England, "has decreed otherwise."

"Curious, sir. What color was his dress when he did so?"

The courtroom burst into laughter, and the prisoner, Butterworth, banged his table with wide-eyed delight. The Queen's cousin, Lord Cornbury, had governed the colony for only a short time, but his open fondness

43

for wearing women's clothing had made the rounds soon enough. Hamilton ignored the question.

"Not that you saw him yourself, of course," Willit continued, turning to the crowd. "We know how busy Cornbury is governing New York and his own benevolent 'Ring of policy.'" The mob broke into disapproving whistles and chaotic discussion. The Cornbury Ring, a collection of politicians the Royal Governor had assembled for the sake of grabbing land, looting public funds, and trying to disenfranchise the New Jersey Quakers, provided plenty to discuss. Riding the tide of the growing outrage, Willit whipped his head back toward Hamilton. "You're not welcome here!" he shouted over the noise and half the crowd cheered in response. Butterworth looked about in amusement.

"Order!" Hamilton shouted back, his face white with fury. "Order! Bailiffs!" The men moved to take Willit away.

"Easy, friends. I've had my say," Willit said quickly, holding up his hands. "And I'll go quietly now. But mark my words, Governor, and mark 'em well. Any judgment made of Mr. Butterworth should come only from the people of Middletown, the British Admiralty, or God himself. Today hangs with you, sir." He turned and made for the back door amid cheers, laughter, and a few boos that were shouted down.

Butterworth turned back around and shrugged at Hamilton and the rest of the bench.

"Any further outburst," Hamilton warned, pointing into the stands, "will be grounds for immediate arrest." Several of the spectators laughed openly. "Mr. Ward," Hamilton pressed on, "will ye please read the charges."

The Attorney General stood. He had heavy jowls and wore the usual dark robes and a short powered wig that hung somewhat crooked as he struggled to find the document. "The prisoners that are charged are as follows," he paused, then found and read the parchment. "Moses Butterworth." He put the paper back down on his table.

Butterworth spun in his chair, looked about the room, holding out his palms in dismay. "Well, this'll be a short one, then, won't it?"

"Does the accused have counsel?" Hamilton asked above the chuckles.

"Plenty," Butterworth replied. "And none of it any damn good, neither."

Laughter erupted in the courtroom again, and Hamilton gaveled the room back into order. "Sir," he pressed. "Will you be represented by legal counsel today?"

Butterworth looked through the room again. He then turned and smiled. "Nah, Mr. Hamilton. It's just me today."

"Then, if there are to be no more interruptions, let us get on with this unfortunate matter and have the full charges delivered."

The Attorney General stood again. "One," he read in a piercing voice, "that the accused did piratically, feloniously, and in a belligerent manner, appropriate, purloin, and sequester the valuables of seven mercantile vessels."

"Now, now," Butterworth lurched in his chair and lifted his shackled hands, waving a finger at the Justices. "That's a bloody falsehood already, mates. All I e'er done was steal stuff."

"Sit back please, Mr. Butterworth," Hamilton snapped.

"Two, that he did, upon the high seas, just outside the colonies of New Jersey and New York, set upon, shoot at, and take two certain merchant sloops, and did assault Captain James Dobbin and other mariners."

"Ah, 'ell," Butterworth sat again. "Dobbins 'ad it comin', your 'onors. Stupid, 'e was. That one just didn't know when to shut up and fold 'is cards, savvy?"

"That on the high sea, about five leagues from Perth Amboy, he did shoot at and take a schooner commanded by Thomas Spenlow and put Spenlow and other mariners in corporeal fear of their lives."

"Perth? I thought that'd been outside Baltimore." Butterworth scratched his chin and looked into the crowd as if to confirm one way or the other. "Fine, fine, then," he said turning to the Governor and Justices. "Let me assert, 'owever, that it seems to me those men 'ad been in 'corporeal fear of their lives' years before I e'er showed up."

"Four, that about one league from Wilmington, ye did board and enter a merchant sloop called *Anchises*, commanded by Benjamin Dillon, and did steal and carry away the sloop and her tackle."

45

"Is that one not included in the first charge, then?"

The Attorney General balked at the question and looked to Hamilton for guidance.

"No, sir," the Proprietor General said, "It is a separate charge."

"But why not just say eight ships at the top, then, and be done with it?"

"It is a separate charge, sir." Hamilton's voice had gained a hint of emotion.

Butterworth sighed. "So ye say." He looked back at the Attorney General and shrugged. "That it, then, Capt'n?"

"And, five, that he did consort with one William Kidd, also known as Captain Kidd, convicted criminal to the Crown and acknowledged villain of the high seas."

"Consort? Well, we ne'er quite got that friendly, mate. But I'll admit to a wee bit of sailin' with the man and sharing a pint on more than one occasion, sure." Butterworth chuckled, and looked back into the crowd. "'Ow is that old seadog, anyhow?"

"Kidd has been incarcerated at Newgate prison for more than a year, Mr. Butterworth. And shortly," Hamilton smiled thinly, "that same outlaw shall be tried for murder by the Lords of the Admiralty. And, likely, strung from the gallows."

"Well, then." Butterworth shook his head. "I reckon' our drinkin' days are *likely* over, ain't they?"

The crowd chuckled and Hamilton waited for quiet before speaking again. "Tell me, Mr. Butterworth, do ye imagine your Captain Kidd now regrets his ways?"

"'Im? I doubt it, gov'nor. Don't get me wrong. Most pirates is certainly sorry if they be 'anged." Butterworth leaned up on the table. "But, rarely that they was a pirate."

"Indeed." Hamilton nodded to the Justices who made several swift notes. "Any further opening comments, Mr. Butterworth, before the honorable Attorney General begins the prosecution of said case?"

Butterworth pushed back his chair with his legs and stood. "I've made me 'ome in Middletown, sirs. With good friends, and a fine wife."

He nodded into the crowd. A plump middle-aged woman blushed and nervously waved back amid the giggles and prodding of her hat-shadowed friends.

"I pay me bloody taxes and show up to church often enough to keep Reverend Jones satisfied 'e's doing 'is job. I ain't sailed for, what, well, years now, gentlemen. Retired, as they say." He sighed, and held out his shackled hands. "Assuredly, we've all got better things to do today than 'ashin out rumors of an untrammeled youth."

Hamilton said. "These charges are from two years ago, sir."

"That close, eh?" Butterworth gazed to the ceiling, thinking. "Seemed much longer, it has. But," he turned to the Justices, "matured quickly I 'ave, mates."

Hamilton shook his head. "The Attorney General will proceed with the prosecution."

Butterworth shrugged to the crowd and sat down again, shaking his head. The mob muttered just behind. Up front, Hamilton conferred with the Justices to his right and the court clerk. The Attorney General fussed with a small stack of papers. "Mr. Grady," Hamilton urged him to begin.

The Attorney General worked his way to the short stand and lifted a paper to begin reading. But even his first words were lost beneath the snare drum.

The sound came from the back of the courtroom. A fluttering drum roll, sprinkled with random, or poorly timed, single strikes. A young lad, no more than nine, stood at the back of the court, and the thick crowd separated to make way for his entrance down the aisle as Butterworth turned with all the others for a better look. The boy was lost within a blue Royal Navy jacket that hung to his knees, the sleeves folded back behind his elbows and drumming hands. The rhythm slowed, turned into a cadence Butterworth clearly recognized. A capstan shanty for sure, meant for lifting the bloody anchor. The beat was heavy and driving, accented with the practiced clicking of the drum sticks where the ship's chantyman would have called out his lines to lead the drill.

The boy held the rhythm until he'd marched to the center of the courtroom.

Over the clatter and scattered laughter, Hamilton stuck his own gavel and shouted for the bailiffs to arrest the boy. Butterworth studied the drummer, long bangs hanging free in the boy's eyes. The drummer's hands danced before his chest, eyes steady and proud as he stared down Hamilton at the front of the courthouse. Something in that look. Resembled an old mate a bit, he thought, as the bailiffs pushed through the crowd. Louis Wright. He'd mentioned a baby boy once, hadn't he? A final flourish, then the boy punched the snare still with a single loud snap. The crowd clapped and laughed and the undersized drummer bowed once courteously.

The two bailiffs turned to Hamilton to see what they should do, and the governor frowned back, frozen in thought. Not that it mattered. By the time he opened his mouth, the first sword had been drawn.

In the newest outrage to the Justices, several men jumped from their seats to stand on their benches. They waved pistols and cutlasses, shouting curses, threats, and ghastly things about Queen Anne's hygiene. In retort, the entire room suddenly exploded in a tempest of sound and movement.

Gunshots burst out across the courtroom and the excited sound of battle filled the cramped hall. Men dropped from the balconies amid shouts and crashing furniture, arms waving, bodies leaping from the swarm only to vanish again. Swords were rattled and clinked together. Women screamed and fought through the suddenly-clambering bodies. Windows were smashed. Half-filled bottles exploded against the walls in splatters of glass and blood-red wine. Whole benches were tossed through the air.

The two bailiffs who'd come out to arrest the drummer boy had almost vanished into the swarming crowd, throttled with clubs and fists. Three prison guards had lifted bayoneted muskets and stood together against the far wall, cornered by a handful of men who snarled and laughed and carried their own shining swords. One of the Court Justices had managed to free a small pistol from beneath his robes and fired it, unprimed, with a deafening click, to great laughter. He was then smacked in the head repeatedly with the other Justice's boot.

Butterworth, one of the few in court *not* scrambling about like a raving dog, watched it all from the view of his own chair. Slouched back, manacled hands across his tummy, legs outstretched and crossed at the boots, he gazed over the melee as if he were simply sitting by a fire along the shore, boiling clams and drinking ale with his mates.

Bodies pushed clumsily through the open doorway. A few scurried across the floor and overturned benches. Someone screamed, a death cry. Several chairs cascaded from the balcony above, exploding on impact below. There were several more sporadic gunshots and the satisfying smell of gunpowder now drifted thickly about the small room. One woman was helped atop the Attorney General's table, where she danced a short jig, then tumbled gracelessly off the end to cheers and laughter. The Attorney General, meanwhile, was being force-fed some of his own paperwork.

In the mere moments that had passed, the courtroom already lay destroyed. Benches and chairs lay scattered and upturned in uneven piles, the floors covered in glass and splinters of wood. The walls dripped wine and were now pocked with bullet holes. Paperwork floated in the air, carried by the wind that came through the smashed windows and someone had suspended two flags from the upper balcony, a red one with black dancing skeletons over a large cutlass, and a black flag, featuring a large hourglass beside two small hearts and the Death's head. The symbols of Captain Bramwell and Phineus Strange, two pirates hung years ago in Wilmington.

Hamilton, like Butterworth, had remained in his own chair. Unlike Butterworth, however, he was not smiling. He simply watched. He had no weapons, after all, and knew there was little chance of sneaking past the mob unnoticed. They'd be looking for him to make the first move. He imagined, at best, the Jarzey rabble would beat him for some time, or even go for the tar and feathers. Certainly, he'd be kidnapped for ransom.

Even now, one figure, a large man with a long dark beard and knee-high boots, had broken past the guards, and was coming straight towards him. Several dark-skinned men loomed just behind. The Proprietor Governor tapped his robes again, hoping a sword of some kind had magically appeared. It had not, and so still he sat, waiting.

49

The large man tossed his own short cutlass across the table between them with a heavy clang, then pulled up a chair to sit beside Hamilton. The man reeked of sweat, his breath rank with ale, and Hamilton saw now the large gold hoop earrings in both ears, and a row of short daggers in a bandolier across his chest.

"G'day, your Honor," the man said, throwing a long arm around the Proprietor Governor.

Hamilton straightened in his chair, the man's chunky fingers digging into his shoulder. "And to you, mister —"

The man smiled. "Ye can call me The Wolf," he said and pulled him close.

"Well then, Mr. Wolf, my anticipation is that —"

The men gathered around them, scouring through Hamilton's belongings, laughed.

Hamilton cleared his throat. "I hope you and your, your mates, realize what a serious offense this is."

"Offense is it, your Honor?" The man calling himself The Wolf had taken his arm away to pull free one of the daggers from his belt. "Tell me, then, if ye find offense in *this*." He turned the knife slowly. "An honorable man's given a trial where evidence is —" He paused. "What's that word, Bucky?"

"Suppressed, Capt'n."

"Aye, that's the one," he turned back to Hamilton. "Where essential evidences was *suppressed* by the prosecution. In order to protect 'important' backers and 'respected' acquaintances, mind you."

Hamilton stiffened within the pirate's grasp, struggling to keep his eyes off the twirling blade. He glanced about the room. The two Justices had been herded between the Attorney General and court clerk, each stripped of his wig and cloak. Some men now simulated a mock trail for the wide-eyed hostages. "This here was to be a fair trial," Hamilton said at last.

"Perhaps. But what of William Kidd, Gov'nor. What of 'is trial?"

"I can not answer to that, nor will I," Hamilton snarled, "be held accountable for measures taken by the Admiralty Court in bloody London."

"Again, perhaps." The Wolf smiled. "The latter still remains to be visited." He pointed his dagger out towards the courtroom where a small crowd had gathered around two fallen men who lay on the ground, moaning in pain. "Men was hurt today," he said. "Good men."

Hamilton studied the forms on the cluttered floor.

"Who is that then?" The Wolf called out.

"Borden, Capt'n. Richard Borden from Middletown."

"A local lad, no less," the pirate sighed. "Struck down by one of your guards."

"A man doing his duty for Queen and —"

"He gonna make it?" shouted the burly pirate.

"'Ard to tell, Capt'n. Plugged through pretty good, he was."

The Wolf leaned backed. "Such misfortune. Now what can we do?" He stabbed the blade's tip into the table so that the knife stood vertically by itself. "A civic resident of fair Middletown has been stabbed by the bayonet of an officer of the court. This has the makings of cold-blooded murder, it does, your Honor." He leaned back to his men. "Reckon we hold this lot 'til we knows for sure young Borden and the others survive."

"Aye, Capt'n," the answer came back.

"Capt'n is it?" Hamilton's eyes narrowed. "Well, *Captain*, when word of this lawlessness reaches the ears of civilized men, royal troops will surely and sharply return to this courthouse. And you and yours will then, just as surely, pay the fair price of justice. There'll be no deal for hostages. There'll be no leniency for such scoundrels."

"Or *from* them either, your honor." The pirate smiled, grabbing Hamilton's hand. "An Attorney General, two Justices, and the bloody Proprietor Governor 'imself. Your mates will *deal* plenty, my lord." With his other hand, he'd retrieved the dagger from the table. "Or," he deliberately eyed Hamilton's hand, "they'll be gettin' little presents rolled under the front door 'til they do."

"They'll storm the courthouse."

"Did ye know this courthouse began its sad days as a fort built for dear Phillip's war?" The pirate slung his legs up on the desk, grinning. "Ain't that so, Hammer?"

"'Tis so, Wolf," replied one of the other men. "True as death."

Andrew Hamilton, the Proprietor Governor of New Jersey looked over his courtroom. Men had already set to boarding over the smashed windows with remnants of benches. They'd also begun barricading the doors. Several armed lookouts stood posted in the balcony, several more by the front windows. Someone had started a small fire with several chairs in the fireplace. Wine bottles were passed between the men. A game of dice had already begun beside the two wounded men.

The Wolf's chuckle broke into his thoughts. "'Ow long you think men such as these could hold out in such a blockhouse, your Honor?"

"No good can come of this, Captain. When this is over, you and the others will likely be arrested and Butterworth will still be forced to pay for — "

"Butterworth?" the pirate laughed, tapping the table with his dagger. His mates snickered back at him. "Sorry, your honor, but he left some time ago."

Hamilton turned, looked about the room again. His eyes moved over the various faces and men moving about the courtroom.

Moses Butterworth was no longer among them.

"There, there, your honor," The Wolf laid the blade down again in front of Hamilton. "'Ow about I teach ye a little game we lads like to play with the pokers on occasion. To 'elp pass the hours at sea and take our minds off troubles for a spell. After all," he smiled, "this matter here might take awhile yet."

Then he spun the dagger.

NOTES: *The standoff at the Middletown Courthouse lasted five days. During negotiations, many of the men vanished quietly never to be seen again, and those left behind were ultimately assured full pardon for safe return of the hostages. A mob of more than fifty people, a blend of citizens defending the rule of law and genuine pirates who'd sneaked into the crowd to free an old mate, were judged to have started the altercation. The cross-dressing Royal Governor of New Jersey was shipped back to England shortly thereafter, and Andrew Hamilton quickly accepted the position as Proprietor Governor of Pennsylvania. Moses Butterworth was never found again. However, many claimed to have known of a reclusive old man with curious friends who lived peacefully in the Highlands across the bay from Sandy Hook, New Jersey for many years thereafter.*

DEAD IN THE WATER

1720, MARYLAND

Dickens was the first to die.

When it happened, they'd all convinced themselves the *Acheron* was completely abandoned. Her decks were clear when they first came upon the eighty foot schooner bobbing atop the ocean's still current, her sails wind-slack and sagging, the lines and rigging draped like forgotten cobwebs. The warning volley across her bow was ignored. Hails from the stalking *Scorpion* went unanswered.

Later, Captain Auciello would remember that someone, he couldn't remember whom, had voiced the possibility of disease, some seaport plague or virus that might have killed the entire crew. That fear had ultimately been proven half right.

The pirates boarded the ship slowly. First, ten men moved across her bulwarks, crossing the unmoving sea in a simple hop. As no one was on deck to repel them, two would have sufficed as the larger group moved about its usual business. They fastened the ships together, dropped a pair of planks be-tween, secured the sails and rudder. Then, Captain Auciello stepped over the tranquil sea with the second team.

Aboard at last, they found the other pirate ship apparently deserted. There were signs of a great struggle across its decks and into the lower levels, gory evidence of both swordplay and fire, but there were no bodies. Several dinghies had been destroyed, the hulls axed apart, and it appeared as if one were missing.

"Find anyone?" Auciello asked. He wondered some if one of Gov'nah Calvert's ships had come across the *Acheron* and taken everyone prisoner. He doubted it. The colonials had never been so bold before. The Maryland coast lay at least two days off by strong sail. And if so, where was the colonial ship? The wind didn't play favorites. If he couldn't get his craft under sail and moving again, no one could.

"Not yet, Capt'n. They could all be hidin' in the lowers, I 'spose. Only got down to the 'tween decks."

Auciello studied the ship carefully. Eighteen guns. Stripped clean for speed. A pirate's vessel, for sure, and in fine shape except for the minor fire damage. A satisfying addition to his growing fleet. "What's she carryin'?"

"A belly of rum barrels. Some coffee. Rations for another two months at sea."

"Up from the islands."

"Just been to, Capt'n, looks like. Food's fresh."

"Best take it all. The rations will come in handy." His own ship had been floating helplessly without wind for more than a week now. There was no telling how long it might last. As a boy sailing the Equator, he'd once been on a merchant ship stuck for two months in the doldrums. And things had gotten bad. "Organize the men as you need," he said, remembering just how bad. "And be quick about it."

"Aye aye, Capt'n."

A mutiny perhaps, Captain Auciello now imagined, looking over the derelict ship again. Such things often happened in the North American "horse latitudes." Even trusty crews eventually grew restless in a dead sea, impatient, angry. This one had likely gotten tired of waiting for the winds to return, of any hollow words of resolve they'd been fed, and had killed the cap'n and his men, tossed all victims overboard. Taken the smaller boat to escape. It made sense.

Captain Auciello brought the folded telescope from his coat pocket and stretched it open. He was a tall man, lean, with sharp features and black coiled hair that fell halfway down his back. He dressed in black too, a long overcoat that broke at his knees, a silver-wrought blade at his hip. The pirate studied eastward, looking for the missing boat. He found only an infinite lifeless sea. How many more days, he wondered.

Then, someone began screaming.

Angry voices from behind and below. *Frightened* voices. Faded. Somewhere in the lower decks. Shouts and curses followed, escaping through the hatchway from the darkness below.

Auciello, and the other men atop, scrambled to the open hatch. More screeching followed. The sound was ugly, filled with rage. Two men drew cutlasses and made for the opening, but Auciello's hand held them. "Who's down there?" he snapped, drawing his own pistol.

"Dickens, Capt'n. Got a crew of four down with 'im."

"Black Jack," he cursed. "If they wasn't waitin' for us below." He peered down into the 'tween deck shadows, collecting his thoughts, furious that he'd grown so careless.

Before he could think to organize the rest of the men for an assault on the lower decks, however, a face appeared at the bottom of the hatchway.

"Clear out," one of his own men called up. "Comin' up." The sailor, a man called Deshowas, scrambled up the steps towards them, springing into the light and making room for others just behind them.

"What's all the shoutin' about?" Auciello snarled. "What bloody happened?"

"Found one hidin' below, Capt'n." Deshowas's voice was strained as he caught his breath. "Lurkin' amid the bodies."

"What bodies?"

Two more seaman crawled out, one carrying an unmoving bloodied body on his shoulder. The body was Dickens, and he was dead. A fourth sailor followed closely behind.

"Jumped poor Dickie rightly, he did. Bit him just like some animal, I swears. Snarlin' like one too. Didn't he, McDrew."

"Aye," McDrew replied, laying Dickens down and wiping his own brow from sweat as Dickens lay lifeless at their feet. "That he did. S'Blood, did you hear 'im?"

"What bodies, Deshowas?" Auciello repeated angrily.

"Bodies in the lowers, Cap'n. Must be a dozen, I'd wager. Dead as the wind is, Capt'n. Dead as our mate Dickens here." The old sailor looked back down the hatchway. "Wrapped in cloth, they was, and tied down good."

"Tied?"

"Aye. Lashed to the boards like," he paused and chuckled darkly. "Like they was goin' somewhere. Tell you rightly, Cap'n, something bad happen' down there."

Auciello took off his feathered hat, fanned himself in the morning sun, thinking. "Where's the prisoner?"

"Sorry, Cap'n," Deshowas touched the hilt of his own cutlass. "That one be givin' us no choice in that matter. Crazy as the Devil 'imself, he was."

"Disease," Auciello said. "Must 'ave been." He reset his hat with a curse. As a boy, he'd seen the Black Death along the Aegean. "Leave the rest. Get everyone off the bloody ship. See if anything already brought over is salvageable."

"What about the treasure, Capt'n? We ain't found the kitty yet."

"Off the ship. Now."

The men nodded in understanding and sprang to action. Two sailors reached to grab Dickens' still form.

"Leave 'im," Auciello grunted, moving back to his own vessel. "He won't mind."

"Capt'n?" Deshowas looked surprised, shot careful looks of confusion at the others.

Auciello sighed. Dickens had been a fittin' pirate, popular amongst the rest of the crew. His loss would be hard felt, and the men were prickly enough without giving another reason to turn on his rule. "Fine," he snapped. "But his body stays up top for burial by the next bell, see."

"Aye, Capt'n." Smiles of appreciation broke across the gathered faces. Captain Auciello moved away from the men without another thought on the matter, quite confident he'd both appeased his crew and properly maintained his command at the same time. In fact, in the ensuing bustle of his ship's departure, he'd soon forgotten the issue completely.

Aboard the *Scorpion*, the crew skulked about, disappointed in the failed raid, cursing the winds, passing around gossip of what had happened, and rooting through the few crates and barrels they'd managed to liberate.

Throughout, Dickens' corpse lay at the aft deck, stitched into a hammock and weighted with roundshot, waiting for proper burial at sea when things settled down and the whole crew was at hand. It wasn't for another four hours before that happened and someone remembered to finally lay the old seaman to rest. By then, it was too late.

Dickens was the first to come back.

☠ ☠ ☠

Ships are like dead things, floating in spacious open graves. Each day, the decks above fade sickly grey, bone grey, under a callous sun as dry rot and barnacles slither unnoticed from the dark sea beneath to latch upon the hull and feast like crypt things. Sails steadily decay in the winds, salt spray, and rains, becoming more fragile and gnarled with each mile sailed. The canvas thins, crinkles, and splits like old skin until the tatters flutter limply from the masts. Dripping in clammy cold or damp warmth, the ocean's salt covers everything, festers as lines erode, the iron tarnishes, and spars and masts become scoured, splintered. The lower decks forever groan against the ocean's constricting pressure as the hull trembles and strains to stay together against her waves.

Know this: The immeasurable creaks and clatters of any ship are its cries of agony. They are its death throes. And only through strenuous work, daily toil for every man aboard, is that death concealed so that the ship may mimic life another day.

The thing lashed to the mast of the *Scorpion*, however, was not a ship. It could not be stitched or sanded, painted or splinted. It could never be properly swabbed or fared, scraped or oiled. It could not be *fixed*. Its unmistakable death could not be concealed.

Captain Auciello and the others watched it from a safe distance in a loose semicircle around the mast. Leahy had been its name, and it watched them right back.

Or rather, its head followed their movements, tilted at times with interest, mouth snapping in hunger. The eyes themselves had completely rolled back, so that only the whites showed. Its skin was dead grey, and the darkened veins gave it an overall marble look with deep bruises and blotches of rot scattered throughout.

He'd been one of the men that Dickens had got. There'd been three that night. Then, Dickens was killed.

The creature now struggled some against the tight bindings, but the effort was slow and labored. Every physical movement, save the gnashing jaws, seemed a struggle. At times, it simply shuddered. The head lolled back, shoulders and arms twitching against the mast.

The first sailor had died immediately. Dickens' own jaws had seen to that. The other two, Leahy and Hadam, took longer. They'd only been bitten, and it wasn't until the next morning that they were found dead in their own hammocks. Asleep by all reckoning. And Auciello supposed that was fitting. Like Dickens, they'd both awakened.

The sounds it made were the worst of all. There were harsh choking sounds, wet and strangled somewhere deep in its throat. Its cracked black lips slobbered saliva and smacked moist and sticky. Rank breath released in unbroken low moans, and it grunted in noises scratchy and terse, mocking human language. At times, it almost sounded as if it were laughing at them.

"How much longer, Capt'n?" one of the men asked quietly.

"I don't know."

"'E's sufferin', 'e is."

One of the men held his hand out, and its head lunged forward, biting at the fingers. "That thing ain't Leahy," he said, waving his fingers to tease. "Wot we care if it suffers?"

"Killed two men, anyways," another added.

At Auciello's instructions, they'd cornered it carefully, lassoed and tied it into submission. To see it get worse. To see it get better. To see if it had

59

fallen under some sort of sickness or curse. He still didn't know.

"Oughta just roundshot 'is boots and dump 'im in the sea wit' the others, we should."

"Can't," Auciello said turning from the thing and looking over the still sea. At the ship's slow crawl, his charts suggested he was still days off the Maryland coast. With wind, by the next morning, but there was still no wind to be found. "Need to know more."

"What's to know?"

"For others who might 'ave it. With these winds, likely another few days to shore. It might —"

"Others," Kern snapped. "Wot others? There weren't no others."

Someone spoke lowly. "Hadam bit *you*," he said.

"Nobody bit me, you bilge rat! Scratched is all, I was. And, ya don't see me gettin' sleepy, do ya? You sayin' I dead, Deshowas?" He drew the pistol at his hip. "Ever see a dead man shoot somebody?"

"Stay that," Auciello snapped, turning round. The men had all squared off, drawing defensively away from each other. "You were scratched, Kern?"

"Wot of it? The other mates was bit, they was."

"Bit, scratched," Auciello shook his head, casually assessing Kern's position and the drawn pistol. "Could be passed in the touch. Just don't know, mates."

"For all ye know," Kern waved the pistol. "It floats through the air like the bloody plague."

The men stepped back, and more than one crossed himself. "True," Auciello replied quickly. "True. And, if that be, the *Scorpion's* in for a stack of doom. All the more reason to figur' matters out and be keepin' our 'eads about us."

"You ain't lashing me to no mast, capt'n." Kern held the pistol at him and several men drew their cutlasses in response. "Savvy?"

Auciello held his hands out in calm. "No, Kern. Ne'er thought it once. Perchance, a short rest though. We can 'ave you fixin' up one of the store rooms until we — "

"I courteously decline, Capt'n," the pirate smiled, backing away from the others. "If you —"

One of the men dove for him and Kern's gun exploded in a loud burst of smoke. Curses filled the deck as each man checked to see if it was he who'd been shot. After Auciello concluded it was not him, he found one man groaning on the deck, and the others closed in on Kern with their swords. "Back, you scurvy dogs!" Kern had drawn his own blade.

"Kern! Don't—" Auciello reached out his hand, but knew, as did Kern, that it was too late.

Backed against the mast, Kern felt the hot breath against his back first. Hot and wet across his shoulder. The thing that had been Leahy lurched forward, latched onto the back of his shoulder. Began feeding.

Kern's screams filled the sea. More curses and shouts erupted across the deck as several men moved to pull him away. Its mouth was now dark and dripping. Kern lay in a trembling heap, surrounded by the others.

"Clean him" Auciello shouted at them, over the thing's excited groans and growling. "Clean and wrap 'is wounds. Then tie 'im below. If he — If he starts changin', end matters."

"Aye, aye, Capt'n." The man's voice was unsure and trembling, but he dragged Kern's struggling body away with two others.

"Bloody 'ell!" Auciello roared at the half-empty deck. Only the still ocean dared to slap against his hull in quiet reply.

"Capt'n."

He readjusted his feathered hat again, thinking. The men could wait. Kern would have to be — Kern could no longer stay on the ship. Give him his own dinghy, perhaps. Set him off. Maybe, he should take a ship himself to sneak off in the night. Leave the *Scorpion* for good. Maybe. "What is it," he said at last.

"Have a look."

He turned slowly to see what Deshowas and the other men were looking at. The thing at the mast had not gotten better. It had not gotten worse. It was just unmoving. Head wilted over, gore spilled down its chest. It was truly dead.

"Bloody 'ell," Auciello said again.

Roderick Dees had been the only man to escape the *Acheron* alive, and it was another three days before Captain Auciello and his men stumbled upon his doomed craft, the missing jolly boat, stranded in the stagnant waters, its single sail drooping in a windless sea, two oars jutted unequally from either side. Dees's body lay slumped in the bow, dead or sleeping in the midday sun, a modest stash of provisions spilled throughout his small craft. He'd screamed when they first woke him. A dreadful scream. A sound Captain Auciello now recognized all too well.

There'd been more outbreaks, and the crew of the *Scorpion* had split into two halves: those who hid below and those who hid on deck. Neither group trusted the well-being of the other, and both groups had watched their own men transform into something only half alive. Auciello now captained only the group who dwelt above.

They'd learned that the curse ran its cycle in two days. Death, then something else, then dead again. It was passed in the saliva, in the blood, and sometimes, a scratch was enough. Those who'd been bit often hid it before changing. Then, there'd been more killing. The crew was down to fewer than twenty now.

Ten now crowded at the helm, while Dees shivered with a blanket across his sunburned shoulders and a cup of cold split pea broth in his hands. His story came slowly at first, his words scratchy and broken. In time, he told his tale.

"We'd been down in the West Indies for a spell," he said. "Huntin' off Santo Domingo, where we found a fine cove to careen the ship and restock before the voyage north. One of the slave islands. Couple o' mates slipped into town to procure some supplies." He shook his head. "And there was some trouble."

"What kind?"

"Usual," he smirked. "Mates takin' a shine to a few of the local lasses. Couple of Negro girls, this time. Carried 'em back right alongside the stolen fruit and dried beef. Against the lasses' own preferences, 'course."

Auciello nodded grimly. It was a common pirate indulgence.

"Evidently shot one of the locals in the course of matters as well. The whole bloody town came out to the sand then, demandin' the girls and such. Filthy savages they was, Capt'n. Bangin' on drums, wailing in that language. *Houngan, houngan, houngan.*" He imitated their chant slowly, quietly.

"*Houngan,*" Auciello repeated the peculiar word.

"Aye," The cook shook his head. "Heard the word long before. As a younger man, workin' on a slaver on the Middle Passage. Magic man, roughly. Or holy man. Someone as knows the darker arts."

"Witchcraft," one of the men gasped, crossing himself.

"Deathcraft more like, mate," Dees said. "Even the slaves was afraid of these men. Said they talked to spirits, they did. Said they, well, that they could even raise the dead."

Auciello shook his head. "It's madness."

"Ducotel was theirs, their *houngan.* Mr. Ducotel. Dark as the night, this one, face painted o'er with a grey skull face. And strange markings on his arms and legs. Looked like the Vice Admiral of Death's own fleet, he did."

"I'd 'ave blasted that terror first, I would," one of Auciello's men commented and the captain glared for him to remain quiet. "What happened next?" he pressed.

"Well," the pirate sighed, "The *Acheron* still fixed in the sand like a dead whale, and there we was around her, a 'undred pistols drawn, 'alf what we needed. Capt'n tries to cut a quick deal with Ducotel. Guns and a few rum barrels for time to get us back in the water. Then we'd hand back the girls."

Auciello shook his head, wondering what he would do in the same predicament. This scenario could be worked out, surely. This one, he could solve. "Sound enough," he decided. "What'd the Negro say?"

"Ducotel just laughed, he did. Said they'd give us until nightfall to move out, but didn't want anything in return. Then he just marched off with the others."

"Got her back in the water and we're making ready to set sail again when they come back. Mr. Ducotel out before the rest, even more revoltin' than before. The paint glowed now, somehow. Hellish, it was. Well, the Capt'n, he rows out with a couple of the men to hand back the lasses. Then Ducotel did it. He blown something on them."

"Blown something? What, man?"

"Dust, sand. Powder of some kind. The ground bones of children and puffer fish, I've heard. Black magic, it is. *Voudoun*, they call it."

"How is such a thing possible?"

"Don't know, sir. Just know that's right before it all started."

"The men dyin'," said Auciello. "Comin' back again."

His eyes narrowed, studied the crew around him. "And how'd you know that, sir?"

The others stiffened and turned to Auciello. "Because," he said into the heavy silence. "We came upon the *Acheron* nary three days ago now."

"But you didn't —"

"We boarded her. And —"

"Dear, God," the man cried, leaping up. "Why? Why the de'il did you pick me up? You boarded her? Mercy." Men moved to restrain him. "That ship was damned, she was. Do you have any bloody idea what you've done?"

Auciello checked the sails again, slack against the windless sea. "Aye," Auciello replied softly. "I think so."

☠ ☠ ☠

The sounds hammering to enter grew louder and more desperate. Its fists now pounded at the barred door, which rattled and creaked against the escalating assault, and the moaning had become more frenzied. It also sounded as if there were at least two of them.

Six days after finding the *Acheron*, Captain Auciello was the only one left. All the others had died, or changed, and his cabin had become the final refuge. He'd hoped to hold them off until the second day. Then, based on what he'd seen, they would stop moving. They would stop mocking both death or life.

He cradled his reliable blunderbuss shotgun and had stuffed half a dozen pistols into his belt. Each was primed and half cocked when the door finally split. Wood splinters scattered across the room as gnarled fingers frantically tore away the rest of the door. A monstrous face suddenly filled the opening, its eyes bone white and vacant, the skin limp and sallow. Its jaw was stripped of skin, the wide bone and teeth exposed and dripping. He thought maybe it was Fisher, from Boston.

Auciello fired the blunderbuss, the sound deafening in the tiny room, and a cluster of pistol balls and nails blew back the face and whatever was left of the top of the door. Behind the smoke, something screamed. Dark shapes, backlit by the midday sun, moved quickly back into the opening. Auciello reloaded. It was something he'd done a hundred times before, but he found his movements clumsy.

Decayed arms, bruised and peeling, reached through the gap again. They tore the wood fragments aside bit by bit until the door buckled at the hinges, shattered at last. The bone lay exposed at one arm, darkly stained and slick, as the thing shuffled through the breach and fell over the bottom half of the door. From behind, another stumbled into the room over it.

Auciello leapt from behind his table and fired the blunderbuss at the one on the floor. It would not ever move again and he dropped the spent weapon for two primed pistols. The second fell backwards away from the flintlock's blast, then staggered again towards him. The pirate shot the second pistol, then leapt over the still form through the shattered doorway and onto the deck. Outside, the bloodied thing that had been Fisher dragged itself towards him. He loosed two more pistols and fired.

The air was rank with the odor of gunpowder and decay. It was the stink of death. The deck lifted and twitched before him, as he staggered in the other direction in a dreamlike haze. Auciello spilled onto the deck, the spent pistols skidding away from his hands.

Off the bow, in the distance, he thought he saw land. Its dark silhouette stretched for miles. He thought briefly of the last dinghy, then pulled

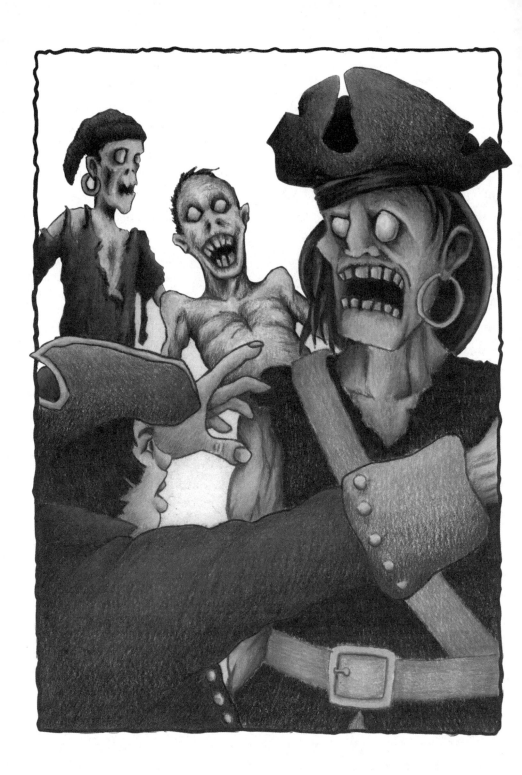

himself to one knee and touched his shoulder.

He felt the sticky gore there, the hot open wound. He remembered the claws digging into his back, fire scorching into his arm. The fantastic agony. His face and neck were still warm and tacky from the previous night. When he'd been bit.

Dark shapes now lumbered towards him from the bow. He made for the hatches of the lower decks.

Down the steps. It was dark below. The lanterns had all burned out, but he knew his vessel from stern to bow and moved easily through the crowded black passages. The horrific reek. Just behind him, something struggled down the steps.

The passages gave way, and the air became thicker with the stench of a tomb. He passed storerooms and the upper bunks. Bodies lay half strewn in their hammocks. Others covered the floor. He could not tell which had been victims and which had — The slow shuffle of a single boot and a bare foot now slapped in the darkness behind him.

He wobbled suddenly, his head dizzier still. Strange images, feverish and angry, continued to fire through his brain. He grabbed a beam to steady himself. The timber felt cold and soft beneath his fingers.

He came at last to the door. Inside, behind lock and key, were the ship paints and oil stores for the lanterns. He fumbled with his keys. His vision felt clouded. He wiped his eyes, hoping to chase away the dark mist. The iron gate opened, and he began unloading the contents.

The oil poured through his fingers, sloshed onto the floor. He opened another and emptied it. More unfamiliar thoughts crowded his efforts. Longing. His thoughts turned to the men back in the hammocks. He grunted against the images that now filled his brain. Kept spilling the oil.

Groans filled the darkness behind him. He dropped the final flask and squeezed his head between his arms. He felt the fire racing from his torn arm, running along his veins to his very brain. The passage filled with the reek of disease. He already smelled it on his own skin. He smelled blood now, too. Not just his own. Auciello lit one of the lanterns with trembling fingers. The passage had grown grey.

Something now stood behind him, and he turned to face his death.

The breath of the thing blew sticky and horrid across his face. It stunk of flesh and blood. Its skin was pale and sunken in the half light, the mouth drawn back in a dripping snarl. Maggots already crawled in what had been the thing's eye. Its bared chest was rotted and moldy. Auciello waited.

But the thing simply stumbled past him into the darkness beyond.

Auciello watched it vanish, heard the moans diminish as it shambled towards the lower levels. He dropped the lantern and the passage ignited. He watched as flames weaved down the oil-soaked passage and the paints caught. The blaze now jumped up the walls. Black oily smoke filled the passageway, and he staggered back towards the hatchway. Every step took effort. His legs felt as if he were walking in the ocean.

At the top of the ladder, he watched the growing smoke lift into the grey sky. It carried on a faint wind. He felt it on his face now. His chest clenched again in agony.

Fire sprouted from the bow, wood crackling in the growing blaze. Timber dried in the sun like an old bone, an unearthed coffin. The flames spit and snaked across the deck.

He staggered to the helm, clumsily lifted his hands to the *Scorpion's* great wheel as he'd done a thousand times before. That alone now carried faint memory for him as the sails whipped and filled against the returning breeze. The wind. He smiled. Then, shuddered with — with *Hunger*.

In the distance, the coast of Maryland. And, several approaching ships. Lord Baltimore's finest. No doubt racing to reach the *Scorpion* and save its crew before the expanding flames completely engulfed her.

With his last human thought, Auciello hoped they were too late.

NOTES: *The southern states lie in a region known to sailors as the "horse latitudes," an area of subsiding dry air and high pressure that creates weak winds wherein sailing ships often stall. Tradition suggests the term originated when Spanish sailing vessels transporting horses to the West Indies often become stranded mid-ocean at this latitude, severely prolonging the voyage. The resulting water shortages made it necessary for crews to throw their horses overboard.*

Although originating in different parts of Africa 10,000 years ago, voodoo, as we know it today, was born in Haiti during European colonization. During this time, the West Indies coffee and sugar plantations imported vast amounts of slave labor from West Africa, and, as a result of their sheer numbers, the slave population was allowed to establish independent social systems and to retain much of its African culture. While zombies are routine fare for Hollywood films (and pirate books!), in Haiti they are taken seriously enough that, even today, creating zombies is a crime punishable by death. While victims do not become blood-hungry monsters, zombies are in fact incapacitated with a powder containing a series of toxic and psychotropic ingredients. The victims become dizzy, their limbs seizing up and their heartbeat slowing to a virtual stop. To all appearances, they are dead. Before the powder kills them completely, however, a voodoo priest will break into their graves and administer the antidote, wherein the victim's mind is largely destroyed and made forever susceptible to suggestion.

LEEDS POINT

1743, New Jersey

It especially liked to watch the boats when there was a storm. That's when they moved most about the big water, when they jumped up and down and splashed. Sometimes, they even broke apart. That was even more fun to see. Men scampered along the tops and ropes and shouted at each other and, now and then, fell into the waves. Then, they would wash ashore or just stay in the dark water forever.

And so, hunched tightly against the harsh storm, wings held close as the driving rain ran past its gleaming blood-red eyes and off its long velvety snout, it watched.

The two hundred ton *Scymetar* tossed within the storm's dark waves like the smallest feather caught in a gusting November wind. In the afterglow of the last lightning flash, the large ship twisted clumsily on her three anchors, rotating in aimless and endless half circles, heeling sharply at each go round as icy water surged over the sloped railings. While spinning, the ship also lifted and plunged, undulating against each furious breaker. One moment, a single wave wrenched the crew thirty feet above the rest of the churning sea; the next, they plunged into the dim below, surrounded on all sides by towering waves.

Many of the lesser spars already lay snapped and twisted within a dreadful tangle of line and masting. Aboard the ship, the loose rope and shredded sail snapped within the tempest winds, and the black pirate flag of Captain Pontus now flailed in tatters, the Death's head lost beneath the driving rain. The crew had hastily rigged preventer shrouds, a temporary brace of extra lines, to support the main mast, which still quivered and creaked against the fervent easterly wind. Most of the cargo, and several of the smaller cannons, had already been cast into the sea. Yet the ship still felt heavy, her hull surely half-filled with water as the sea rose and splashed on all sides, the heavy rain pounded from above.

Somehow, men still scrambled through the torrent, fighting towards the anchor cables. They had no choice. The anchors were dragging. If not cut away, the boat would shortly be smashed to pieces. Cursing and shouts broke through the raucous storm as the men staggered forward. Another wave crashed over the ship's plunging bow in an explosion of spray and sound as the Atlantic surged again over the drenched decks. Two men tumbled back-wards, one slammed into the railings, the other flushed over the side into the roiling sea, his scream gobbled by the wind.

Stephen pressed forward with the others toward the cables, leaning hard against the blustering winds and rain. The boy held his axe tightly in both hands. Closer each step. Lightning flickered again beside the ship, the immediate crack of thunder deafening as the boat tilted hard starboard and cold sea water rushed over his legs. Beside him, the jagged end of a spar that had crashed overboard suddenly lifted from the waves like a great sea mon-ster. He slipped against someone and pitched headlong onto the flooded deck. Brackish water rushed over his face and into his mouth.

"Get up!" a voice shouted above. "Get the bloody bowers cut!" Ste-phen fought to his legs again to straddle the belt cable and second anchor. He struck once, then moved away quickly for another man's axe to chop. Men shouted back from the other cables as their dark shadows hewed and stumbled. Stephen's axe fell again and one of the cable's four cords broke away. The boat swayed and he tottered sideways, fought back to his position and swung the axe a third time. He stopped mid-swing at the fourth.

He'd just seen it again.

There, against the flash of lighting, moving back and forth along the shore. The creature. The demon. He'd heard the other men talking. Almost human, yet he could see what looked like wings.

"Don't look at it!" MacKinnon snarled beside him. "Finish the job."

Stephen swung down again, the axe driving into the deck with a wet crack and the cable cut free at last, vanishing through the hawsehole. Cold water spewed over his back and he clung to the half-buried axe to hold himself steady.

"Clear!" the captain shouted behind them over the wind. "Clear the bloody deck!"

Stephen freed the axe and stumbled back with the others. They hurried over the sloshing decks. With the anchors cut, the *Scymetar* already moved more naturally within the waves, pitched back and forth, wedged between the shore and the deep ocean.

Many in the crew retreated just outside the main cabin, huddled together, wet through and shivering. Cursing, and some praying too, between breathless pants. Another thirty worked the buckets and hoses as the pumps were flooded, along with the galley and oar compartments

"Little to bloody do but wait it out," Captain Pontus said. He wiped the rain from his shaved head. "If pushed out, we live. Pushed to shore — Who's lost already?"

"Rucker. Gould. Oily John."

"What of Clifton? Will he —"

"'Is head be 'holly crushed by the fallen gaff, Capt'n. 'E's a grave man for sure."

Another man cursed. "We'll all be crewing for Davy Jones by the morning, mates."

The captain cuffed him. "There'll be none of that, ye weedy worms. The *Scymetar's* a fine old hag who's bedded far worse than this. Go sound the well again!"

Quimby's voice cut in, high and thin. "And what about that thing, Captain?"

"The Leeds Devil, I know 'tis."

"'Tis nothing," Captain Pontus growled, his voice brooking no argument.

"Devil? What devil ye say?"

"Sea dragons and mermaids next!" Pontus glowered and reached instinctively for the pistol at his hip. "Enough of the drunken myths, fools. I'll not 'ave it on me ship!" Thunder and lightening exploded behind him as he spoke, lending authority to his words.

"That be Leed's Point," Splinter said anyway, pointing out to the shore and ignoring the captain's curse. He no doubt knew Pontus's gun powder was soaked through and would not fire anyway. "A cursed place. Damned by Old Horney 'imself."

"Cursed?" Fletcher crossed himself. "*Jesu*. You say 'cursed,' no?"

Splinter shook the rain from his coat as Captain Pontus grumbled behind them. "Witchcraft, I've heard," he said. "One of those Leeds women gave birth to a demon child. Looked a regular brat at first, I've heard. But, then it changed." He looked at the men gathered around him. "Changed into something quite — unnatural."

"Is it human then?" one of the men asked.

The pirate shrugged in the rain. "Only God dare answer that, Fletcher."

"And you can ask 'im yourself, soon enough, mate," one of the crew gruffed.

Splinter smiled. "It 'as the face of a 'orse, they say. And the serpent's tail."

Stephen looked across the ocean, but could not see it anymore through the rain. Did it really have the head of a horse? Was such a thing even possible? He'd seen the "mermaids" and "dragons" the seaman occasionally sold on the docks. Real sea monsters they called 'em. But he'd learned they was all "Jenny Hanivers." Fakes. Grotesque figures formed simply from dried-out skates and mantas. Yet, the thing he'd seen tonight had moved. It had fluttered its wings.

"And wings," Stephen added softly.

"Aye, young woodworm. That 'e does. Flies just like a crane. Picks the man right off the deck. 'Eard it killed its 'ole family the cursed night it be

73

born. That it commonly feasts on children, savvy." Splinter half-lunged at Stephen, laughing.

"And sinks ships for fun," MacKinnon said.

"Aye," Splinter turned. "That too, excellent MacKinnon. Attacked a Dutch square-rigger just outside of Great Egg Harbour last summer. Killed every man aboard."

"They say," MacKinnon continued. "If you listen close enough, men will hear it laughing. Laughing as they drown."

The crew grew silent, turned to the strange shape on the shore. Each man listening for its morbid cackle over the rain and wind. Stephen listened too, and secretly hoped with all his heart that he would hear nothing. Some strange sound on the wind, though, almost like singing.

"We'd best free the carpenter," Stephen said suddenly. "The lodgings is flooding."

"Who?"

"The man tied below."

"Aye, forgot 'bout that sniveling squid in all the excitement, don't ya know." The captain shook his head. "'E's as good as dead anyway. 'Eard Rucker, may his pitiful soul rot below, 'it the man too 'ard again."

"Aye, that he did, Capt'n."

"Well, then, if that don't kill him, the water surely will. 'Twas surely a bad night to join the crew of the *Scymetar*."

"Capt'n, wot if he ain't dead yet?" Stephen asked. "He'll drown."

"Then go and bloody free 'em, laddy!" He kicked at the boy. "But the damn lowers is 'alf flooded already, so din't expect none of us to bloody come and save ya."

Stephen shuffled away, held the curse under his breath. He paused at the hatchway to take another peek at the creature. It had moved. Come off the natural dunes to prance across the dark beach. The large shadow almost looked as if it were hopping. Dancing.

74

The sand felt cool and wet. Soft. It felt good under its heavy hoofed feet. Look-ing out, the big water stretched for miles in every direction. It was etched black, almost as black as the cellar where the mother kept it before its escape, and the loud light flashed in jagged beams from a half dozen different spots within that darkness. It was good. The waves crashed loudly over the shore, pushing water up to the sandbanks to swirl over its feet. The creature splashed and danced in the cold water. Just ahead, in the waves, the big boat danced with it.

☠ ☠ ☠

Below deck, the man sat still, unexpectedly conscious, hands still tied behind his back and lashed to a post. His pants and shirt were wet and the sea water ran this way and that across his legs and over the slick floor. There was a large wine-colored welt on the left of his forehead where Rucker had knocked him with the club. They'd thought Rucker had broken his skull, killing yet another conscript by mistake. The blood had dried and dripped across his cheek and collar. He'd paid no notice to Stephen's approach, but the boy still stepped forward carefully.

"Your ship's breaking apart," the man said.

Stephen jumped at the voice. The captive turned to look at him. He looked to be about thirty. Black hair curled at his shoulders. His eyes were blue and fierce with rage, which was understandable. Only hours before, he'd been beaten, robbed, and taken against his will.

"We just cut the anchors away," Stephen said.

"Don't matter. Listen." The man turned his head in the darkness. He'd winced when he moved. "Hear that?"

"The hull."

"More specific, boy."

Stephen listened to the *Scymetar*, the ship that had been his only home for the last two of his fourteen years. He heard the monstrous waves slapping against the sides of the whole, the muted thunder. The sideboards yawning open, squeaking, dripping. He heard the water heavy and sloshing in the lower hull. Then, another sound, a profound moan half-muffled by the water.

75

"The keel," Stephen said at last. "One of the frames is chafing against it."

"Aye, good. From stem to sternpost, she's the backbone of every ship. And she's breakin' away from the frames. I've heard 'em snapping. There's too much damned pressure on the hull."

"Right."

"What's your name, boy?"

"Stephen Rawlins. I'm the carpenter's mate."

"I see." The man sighed. "Well then, Mr. Rawlins, where are we?"

"Just off Brigantine. Placed called Leeds Point. Aboard the *Scymetar*." Stephen crouched to untie the knots which held him.

"Pirate ship."

"Aye."

"You'll get no ransom for the likes of me. And, I have no money to —"

"No, we —" Stephen paused. "One of the men heard you talkin' about that job in Wilmington."

The man smiled, shook his head. "I see. You needed a carpenter."

"Aye. Ours was lost in the last boarding." He finished untying the knots.

"So, let me see if I have the mark," the man shook the lines free and rubbed his rope-bruised wrists. "Instead of reporting for work at Lengerich Boatyard for lodgings and two pounds a month, I've been gangpressed at the end of some bully's club to work aboard a depraved pirate ship. Is that it?"

Stephen backed away, afraid to answer. Many in the crew had started as men from captured ships forced into service. Such men adapted to the matter, eventually welcomed it, or were easily discarded. Skilled carpenters and navigators were of especially high demand, and this one would be given extra time and incentive to adjust. If he lived.

If any of them lived.

The man touched the gruesome wound at his head softly, scowled in discomfort. The ship groaned then. The terrible noise rumbled beneath their feet.

"Too much pressure on the hull," Stephen echoed the man's earlier words, watching him rise.

"Aye."

"We should cut the masts," the boy said.

"We should."

"Does that mean you'll help?"

"It does."

Parker, the name the man gave the captain, stood with Stephen and several other men, hewing at the *Scymetar's* mainmast with axes. The mizzen and fore had already been chopped down, discarded in smaller pieces into the furious sea. Every so often, one of the men would stop and sneak a peek back towards the shore.

"Keep hackin', ye dung flies!" Captain Pontus surveyed the job, arms crossed, his protests and face half lost in the driving rain. "Bloody 'ope ye know what you're doing, Parker," he grumbled. "Or your career with the *Scymetar* will be the shortest ever."

The man laughed. "And, to think, I was just warmin' up to the place." He swung the axe again. "Captain, if we don't release the strain on her hull, none of your threats will matter. You, and your filthy crew, will be right beside me." He stepped back for others to move in. "If it ain't too late already..."

The mast split and Parker waved the men back. The crew stepped away as the weight of the mast and the wind took care of the rest. The cut widened, the piercing, cracking sound cutting through the storm, and the mast snapped away from itself. The shroud lines they'd purposely left secured led the enormous pole sideways, where it crashed through the port railings. Men immediately set to chopping the mast in smaller sections. Stephen joined them. No sense arming the sea with such a weapon to be later tossed back at the ship.

"Fine work, men," Pontus shouted.

Parker wiped the water from his face, grimaced in pain. "If she runs aground, captain," he said. "She'll probably still go down. You got a hold packed with nothing but water and several loose frames already."

The captain studied the new man, their eyes locked with irritation across the rain. Stephen could almost feel the two using their mutual dislike to find strength, to focus, to think, and just maybe figure out another way to survive a few minutes more.

"When she does, your men will run to the launches and cockboat," Parker said, looking about the ship. "Don't let 'em. They're death traps. They'll load too heavy or too light and the —"

"Indebted, Parker. Now, how 'bout ye get below and think of a way to get rid of some of that water you're so fearful of." The ship lifted again on a fat wave and the Captain stumbled ahead to the forecastle.

Parker stood motionless on the deck staring out absently at the sea. For the first time, Stephen thought his eyes seemed cloudy, unfocused. "Sir," he spoke up. "Are you — "

"Head hurts is all," Parker said, looking at Stephen and coming back from where his mind had wandered. "Took quite a wallop, I understand."

"Aye," the boy said. He waited a beat. "We're being swept ashore."

"Yes."

"The keel's already hit bottom."

"You felt that too?"

"Smaller rafts might work. Each man gets his own."

"They might. Do you know why?"

Stephen thought. Lightning flashed beside the ship. "No," he said in the after rumble.

"You should. The key to buoyancy is how much volume the object displaces compared to its weight."

"So a craft built to carry my weight should stay afloat, stay upright."

"Aye. If you keep out the water weight. The rain."

"You'd get pulled out to sea."

"Maybe. Or pushed ashore. A small anchor dropped at the breakers will make sure you don't go out to sea."

"So, we need weight and a small boat."

"I was thinking a small cannon and an emptied grog barrel."

"Oh, we got plenty of both."

"I thought you might," the man grinned in the rain.

"What about —" Stephen turned to the beach, looked to where the shadowed figure hunched over something. Dragging something up the beach. "What about that thing?"

Parker was already moving for the hatches.

☠ ☠ ☠

It pawed at the dead man. The one who'd washed ashore beside the pretty bottles and some broken wood. He didn't move, except for the one booted foot that swayed from side to side awkwardly in the lively tide. Face in the sand, body bloated with water. It leaned closer to smell the ocean and sweat. Poked at him. Cold and slick as a fish. Like others he'd found before. Rolled him over. Waves frothed up the man's twisted body and yanked at the legs to pull him back into the big water again. Its taloned hand grabbed hold of the dead man's shirt and sharp nails stabbed into the wet cloth, slashed into cold skin. Heavy, but not too heavy. It dragged him back towards the sandbank.

☠ ☠ ☠

They finished a fifth escape craft. It was an emptied port barrel rigged with an undersized keel, canvas lashed over the top to keep out the water and rain. Stephen had nailed wood blocks into his to add the appropriate weight. They'd attached a hundred feet of cable to it and had lashed the other end to the ten-pounder cannon.

"Best to use a chain hitch on that."

The boy quickly tied the knot, ignoring the numbness in his cold, wrinkled fingers.

"You do good work," the man told him.

Stephen nodded, and moved for another barrel. There were seventy-nine men aboard the ship. "Thank you, sir."

"When we get out of this, perhaps you could – "

"Maybe, sir."

The man reached for their shared mallet. "How'd you end up with this lot, anyhow?"

"Was a hand on the *Shepherdess*, a merchant ship out of Baltimore. My brother and me."

"He with this lot too?"

Stephen shook his head no. Paused, his head swarming with memories.

Before the man could ask him more, the *Scymetar* finally ran aground. The whole ship jolted, rolled sideways against the reef of sand in one abrupt movement that signaled its death.

Stephen heard her hull split. Shattered against the impact. Parker was right, it had been too late. Cutting the masts hadn't been enough. The hull was too weak and the entire right side of the *Scymetar* collapsed.

Planks fractured and jutted oddly away from the ship. Sea water rushed over her railings, swallowing the deck, washing out a dozen men in a single sweep that reached the stump of the mainmast. The ship lay tilted, the waves pounding it deeper against the sand reef, threatening to turn her over. Screams filled the *Scymetar* now as men tumbled into the sea or scrambled for the smaller boats.

An enormous wave crested over the port side, flushing men from the lesser boats across the deck to the other side. Bodies thrashed in the water, surrounded by wreckage, and others still struggled at the launch boats; wrestling to free them while the ship slammed sideways against the sand.

Stephen and Parker rolled the cannon towards the main deck. The wheels moved slowly, each inch earned with effort. He saw that the wound on Parker's head had opened again, running dark against the sopping wind that streaked across his face. Behind them, a dozen men had managed to free one of the boats and had it lifting and plummeting in the waves beside the *Scymetar*, crashing against its hull. Several were already in the dinghy when it tipped, pulled under a wave's crest and forced beneath the ship.

"We can save three more," Parker said. His voice sounded odd. Slow. Before Stephen could say anything, the man waved him away. "Best pick 'em now," he said. "She's breaking up."

Stephen did as he was told and dashed forward over the debris of tackle, cables, and cookery that swished this way and that on the water between his boots. The ship had lifted oddly, bow towards the black-shrouded heavens, and many of the other men had gathered underneath the foremast stump to escape the ever-rising sea. Hard rain battered his face and the lifting tide rushed over his boots.

Just ahead, the crew tousled and argued over the last two launches. Stephen found he'd stopped running.

He watched as MacKinnon, fighting onto a launch with his fists, was purposely pushed overboard by two other men. Lightning flashed. Someone had drawn a sword and Fletcher was stabbed through. Bundles and goods were tossed into the skiffs. A year's worth of booty gone, most of it spilling off the deck into the churning sea.

Another boat was free in the water, several men pulling hard at the oars. Captain Pontus himself worked the tiller.

Stephen watched only a moment more. The captain and his crew of nine struggling against the tide as it fell away. He thought of his brother. And, his own last two years. The *Scymetar* shook under his feet, trembling against the ocean floor. Then, he decided. There was only one man left to save.

Screams suddenly broke behind him.

As he turned, Stephen heard something new in the whooshing wind. Something he'd not heard before, but a strange high sound slipped between the low moan of the wind. Rhythmic. It almost sounded like a large bird flapping its wings.

He looked up just as the black form passed overhead. He had not really seen it. Not yet. Only a glimpse of an enormous dark shape, something larger than any man he'd yet met. It moved past him with animal speed. The silhouette of jagged wings spread out on either side, wide and blocking out the dark sky above. When it passed, a pair of hairy legs and a long tail trailed behind.

The creature landed just behind the men and now clung to the front of the ship like a giant bat, hunched over the bowsprit, wings spread out in the darkness. Stephen stared silently in the rain as the thing began its slow crawl down the pole towards the arguing men.

Now, he could see it clearly. The Leeds Devil.

And it wasn't the sea yarn of some drunken pirate or a "Jenny Hanivers" sea devil carved to fool the landlubbers. *It was real.*

The face was stretched, extended into the monstrous snout of some hideous barnyard animal. An ox or horse. The skin seemed dark, patched in course brown hair with several long black strands straggled over its malformed forehead. Its eyes were blood-red slits that glowed like the embers of a faded bonfire.

Someone finally turned and shouted. Men screamed. Cutlasses were drawn. A lone pistol shot rang out in the wind. Some jumped into the water to escape it. Others scrambled away over the deck, running straight towards Stephen.

The creature shrieked. The sound was a high-pitched warble that lasted several seconds and cut through the storm like the very trumpets of Hell. Stephen held his hands to his ear and cringed in fear before the horrible noise. Water dripped off the tangled body and pooled under its grotesque shadow. The Leeds Devil pounced onto the deck.

Several men shoved past Stephen, cursed his name, and he turned after them, stumbling backwards himself. Dark water overran the side of the deck. He slipped and slid through it and made his way back to Parker.

Parker lay perfectly still, slumped over the cannon as if he were sleeping. It seemed Rucker had hit him too hard, after all.

Stephen watched the ocean for a moment, then gently moved the body aside.

The cannon splashed into the sea and quickly vanished into its black depths. It had only taken twenty feet of rope before hitting the shallow rand reef somewhere below. Stephen tossed the line after it, then cut away the other barrels. There was no one else. The ship shuddered violently, the quarterdeck breaking away into the ocean at last. Planks and pole snapped and shattered in a sound that completely consumed the din of the storm.

His barrel fell into the sea. Stephen crouched inside and it landed with a dull thud and shocking collision as pain raced up his legs and back.

Water spilled into the top and he quickly adjusted the canvas. He could feel it floating, bobbing in the violent waves. Peeking over the barrel's edge, he found the keel of the last launch tipped over. Several men struggled beside it, the waves crashing over their dark shapes. The captain was no longer among them. There was no one left to see him when the barrel rolled on the next wave over the reef.

The *Scymetar* bucked and buckled behind him now. It had turned on its side, the starboard lost under the raging water. Waves crashing over the top. Several shapes moved within the wreckage, vanishing with each new wave.

Atop the rubble and timber shards, perched over what was left of the forecastle like some great bird of prey, the creature sat and flailed its great wings. It shrieked again in the darkness. The sound was answered in a double crash of thunder.

Stephen turned away from the thing, away from the crumbling *Scymetar*, and settled back into his own "ship." Safely on the right side of the reef, the barrel was moving towards shore after all, and he cut the safety line.

Time stretched and bent with the ocean's nearly-spent fury. While drifting ever closer towards shore, Stephen thought about a man called Parker. A good enough name to use himself if he happened to find his way to Wilmington, and a place called Lengerich Boatyard. They'd be expecting a carpenter, he thought, and hoped Parker wouldn't mind. Much later, Stephen liked to imagine, he'd have even approved the idea.

He spilled from the barrel and started swimming for shore.

☠ ☠ ☠

It watched the boy climb from the funny little boat and swim for the shore. The waves tugged and pushed at the boy's small shape, threatened to drive him under or drag him again into the big water. The boy was strong. He kept swimming. It thought of following him, of flying over the waves again and playing with the boy. But there was still more to see out in the water. The big boat was sinking into the sand. Falling into many pieces. Many men floated within.

On shore, the boy now stood on the beach, staring out at the big boat. Rain fell on him. His shape was small and black against the storm. When he finally turned to run from the beach, he looked just like the smallest feather.

The creature laughed at the thought, and the sound carried away on the swirling winds.

NOTES: *The Leeds Devil was renamed the Jersey Devil by the big city newspapers in 1909, when the creature allegedly left its infamous home along the shore's Pine Barrens to briefly romp through Philadelphia and several major suburbs of New Jersey. During that occasion, the strange being stepped from New Jersey folklore dating back to the early 1700s and was reported to have been spotted by hundreds of witnesses. While the myth of the Jersey Devil has not yet gained the fame of such beings as the Northwest's Big Foot or Scotland's Loch Ness Monster, its legend, and the notion that it still roams those dark woods daring to be found, has thrived across the Middle Atlantic for almost three hundred years. It is commonly held that the creature enjoyed watching, and perhaps causing, shipwrecks. For years, sailors along Jersey's shores feared that possibility.*

SKULLS AND STRIPES

1776, VIRGINIA

The foreign spy schemed from the tavern's back table, its rough, heavy wood hung with the veil of many years' shadow and smoke. Two men, pirates by dress and manner, sat across from him. "In essence, *messieurs*," he spoke in the muted words of such places, "You shall continue to hunt *l'Atlantique* and any spoils found within are respectfully yours to keep, less five percent."

"Then, in essence, mate —" one of the two smiled, his words somewhat slurred with the ale. "— you offer what we already got, less five percent."

The spy, who called himself Beaumarchais, waived away the barb as if chasing away the bad smell from the room, then pulled documents from inside his dark cerulean coat and slid them across the table. "My good man, if you are captured now, you will be charged with piracy and swiftly executed. *Fini*. Conversely..."

The second pirate reluctantly took the paper and read slowly. "Is hereby granted the authority to subdue, seize, and take any armed or unarmed enemy vessel, public or private, which shall be found within these Atlantic waters, or elsewhere on the high seas, and such captured vessel, with her apparel, guns, and so on and such forth." He glanced up. "You *want* us to be pirates?"

"Your 'Letter of Marque,' *mon ami*." Beaumarchais casually smoothed the dark scarf around his neck. "Your unique livelihood legalized with the stroke of this quill. You attack only my colleagues' enemy, and there will be no interference from the native law. In fact, safe harbor and supplies will now be made available to your crew in a dozen different ports up the coast. A greater chance of freedom to better challenge your particular talents. I need merely write your names atop."

"What about them guns?" the first pirate asked, his voice lowered even more beneath the crowd. "You said something about smuggling guns for extra."

Beaumarchais smiled. "Perhaps." he nodded. "In time."

"And what do we do with the ships when we catch 'em."

"You're pirates, *monsieur*. I'm sure you will think of something." Beaumarchais waved his hand again. "Burn them if you wish or keep them for yourselves. It matters not to the men I speak for." He leaned back in his chair into the darkness, and folded his hands to wait as the two men studied the paper for some time, and argued between themselves, their speech half filled with curses. "*Oui?*" he asked at last.

"Why not." The pirate tapped his colleague in the chest.

Beaumarchais bowed respectfully, dipped the quill, and proceeded to fill in the information at the top while the two men downed their ales and sneered at the rest of the room.

"There," he said, putting aside the quill. "You have joined an extraordinary moment in history, *messieurs*."

"How grand." The first pirate wiped his mouth with the cuff of his sleeve and grabbed the paper from the table. "We're done here, then? We've got huntin' to get to, mate." He elbowed his partner again and the two men staggered through the tavern and out the back door.

"*Morbleu*," Beaumarchais swore and rubbed the back of his neck. If this were the best he could find, his cause was lost. The enemy would surely win.

He leaned sidewise, addressed the shadowed man who sat at the table adjacent to his own. The man who'd been eavesdropping throughout the conversation, the one he'd really been speaking to the whole time. "And what of you, *monsieur?*"

This man was olive skinned with sharp features and dark hair pulled into a short ponytail. Of Spanish descent, perhaps. There was a tattoo of a dragon or sea serpent on his right forearm, the sun-faded ink trailing up into his black cotton shirt. He sat alone, observing the room like an angry hawk, and turned his critical gaze on Beaumarchais. "And the guns?" the man asked quietly.

"Up from the Caribbean, *monsieur*. You would be paid for each shipment above and beyond the spoils you and your men harvest between."

"And we are free to steal and kill as we see fit."

"*Oui*."

"I'll have to talk to my crew first," he said. "But if the money's right, they may be amendable to the idea." He stood up from the table, lean and angular, a cutlass hung at his side, a pistol at his waist. He fixed Beaumarchais with a final appraisal. "And who, exactly, are we pirating for, *monsieur*?"

Beaumarchais smiled. "These United States of America, of course."

☠☠☠

From the quarter deck of the *Klymene*, Captain Roarke watched their latest prize. The British merchant ship, a fifty-foot sloop bound for the North with supplies for the redcoats, had been found and chosen thirty miles out. Fifteen men, perhaps. One swivel gun against his crew of a hundred and ten and twenty-six working cannons. The *Klymene* had given chase for more than an hour as the guns were rolled out, the decks sanded, and the bulwarks taken down for the impending boarding. On opposite tacks, the two ships now closed along the lines of an enormous obtuse angle.

Roarke leaned against the deck's rail with his arms crossed beneath the late afternoon sun. Hands were aloft releasing the last bit of sail. Only a matter of minutes, now. "Port your helm, Mr. Jones. Keep her as near the wind as she'll lie."

"Aye, Captain," the steersman replied.

"Take in two reefs at the tops'ls!" Roarke called out, squinting at the men above. "Won't be long, men!"

As he spoke, Hotchpotch, the ship's quartermaster, pounded up the steps towards him with his customary heavy stride. A large man, with long jowls and a short rust-tinted beard, he had several weathered pistols jammed into his belt. Roarke smiled, doubting the guns were even loaded. Even his men knew it would be another simple capture. Hotchpotch tossed something at him.

"What's this?" said Roarke.

"For when we 'oist our colors, Captain."

"We've already got a flag, mate." He nodded above to where the *Klymene's* notorious flag whipped behind the ocean's winds. It was black, per the custom of the vocation, and adorned with the side view of a flexed arm holding a cutlass. Small alternating suns and moons ran along the top of the flag, and matching skulls lined the bottom. "She's flown over this ship for two years now."

He shook open the flag that Hotchpotch had just thrown him, and held it out. It was the same flag the colonies had lived under for his entire life, the red British ensign flag with the Union Jack in the left corner. Only someone had sewn white stripes across the red, six white stripes.

"It's the new colors, Captain. General Washington designed it himself and 'is troops 'ave been marching under it all year."

"Washington, eh?" Roarke still watched the closing merchant ship, rechecked its line. "Starboard a point, Mr. Sullender."

"Aye, Captain."

"There's thirteen stripes now, see," Hotchpotch said, taking the flag back. "One for each colony."

"So, I gathered." He noticed several of the other crew members were listening and glanced at their own black flag again. "You seem fairly certain the Colonials will win this scuffle, old friend. Yet, your celebrated flag maker and his men were thrashed at Long Island and have since been completely chased out of New York. Do you really want their flag flying from our mast when the Redcoats finish the job?" He'd lifted his telescope to better see the other ship.

"One battle don't matter none. It's bound to 'appen, Captain. The King's a right tyrant, 'e is. And there ain't no way a little island can rule a whole continent. Just don't make no sense."

"Yes." Roarke smirked, "Mr. Paine suggested you'd think so."

"That the new cook's mate, Captain?"

"Never mind," he lowered his telescope and moved towards the gangway. "Stow that cursed flag and rouse the boarding teams. Mr. Reed!"

"Aye, Captain?"

"If you would be so kind, put a shot across her bow. The King's a tyrant, evidently, and it seems only fair we take his property."

☠ ☠ ☠

Beaumarchais did not look well. The French spy's usual fuss and pallid color were particularly noticeable as he pushed past the other men and clambered at last aboard the *Klymene*. Below the ship's chains, several launch boats, just loaded with French muskets and powder the *Klymene* had carried up from the Caribbean, started again for the Virginia shore. Another successful run for the crew. Roarke had been surprised at how well the men took to such work. Hotchpotch wasn't the only man on the crew stirred by the colonial effort, and it had been a surprisingly fruitful autumn in the cold northern Atlantic. Twenty boats captured in just three months. Three deliveries of armaments for the colonials. "*Monsieur* Beaumarchais," Roarke greeted the Frenchman amid the bustling crew.

"Forget the rest of the supplies," Beaumarchais gasped, straightening himself at the aft. "We must depart at once."

Roarke looked quickly about the harbor. Saw no suggestion of trouble. "Why?" he asked. The men had already begun loading another boat.

"We must speak privately." He moved to pull Roarke aside.

Roarke stayed his ground. "The money."

"*Mon Dieu!*" Beaumarchais shoved the bag into his hands. "Now, there is no time." The Frenchmen took off his black tricorn hat, caught his breath. "My personal delivery today is not by chance, *Monsieur*. I was to meet someone here. A colleague shortly destined for France, who has been captured. A principal American patriot."

"And we're to —"

"Pursue the Britons, naturally and liberate him. The *Klymene* is the fastest ship for a hundred miles, and the providence of the Great Maker has surely brought you here today for this reason."

Roarke shook his head. "That's not what we do, *Monsieur*." He tossed the bag of gold coins to Hotchpotch, who would allot it among the others later.

"But you must! This is an influential man in your war for independence. If he is taken to England, it will be humiliating, disastrous for the colonies' international reputation. Also, he will likely be hanged as a traitor!"

"Regardless, it is still not what we do. It's not *our* war for independence. And your request is absurd. How would we even find them? The Atlantic is wide, *monsieur*. Even you must be aware of that."

"They left only hours ago on an easterly wind. A frigate. A large and slow ship, for sure."

Roarke frowned. "A bloody man-o-war," he murmured.

"*Oui*," Beaumarchais admitted. "The *Temperance*."

"I know her. She's a two decker with fifty guns. It's a fool's errand, man. How much will you pay? No, never mind, it matters not."

"I have none to give you now. I am sure reward money would be collected —"

"I said it matters not."

The Frenchman's eyes had narrowed angrily. "He is also my friend, *Monsieur* Roarke."

"Then I offer my sincerest sympathy to you, sir," said Roarke. "But that is all I will offer. I can not risk this crew for an ill-fated mission of mercy."

"Isn't that for your men to decide themselves? Is that not your code?"

Roarke's first impulse was to throttle the raging Frenchman with the hilt of his cutlass, and his own anger surely showed, for the spy had taken a step back.

"Am I to presume, sir," Beaumarchais said, straightening, "that you are no patriot, no admirer of the Maker's cry for true democracy."

Roarke sneered. "The same democracy that murdered Socrates and Christ? The democracy that Plato feared and your own Rousseau even now proclaims impossible? 'So perfect a government is not for men.' All men may be *created* equal, *Monsieur*, but they do not finish so. Democracy demands conditions too numerous and virtues too difficult for the whole. I shall never trust a mob."

"Yet, sir, you trust your own men."

Roarke spun away from the conversation, slammed his fist against the railing. "I presume you would continue to speak even after I cut out your tongue." He turned back, touched the dagger at his hip. "I wonder..."

Beaumarchais had crossed his arms, and now rolled his eyes to the sky. "*Abruti.*"

"Hotchpotch!" Roarke gritted out.

"Captain?"

"Gather the men at the main deck, straight away. We have matters to discuss."

In the space of mere minutes, it was decided. The first few hands rose immediately. The rest came more slowly, but spread gradually across the deck until Roarke could no longer see over them. One of the men, Skelly Brown for sure, had raised his gleaming hook into the air. Then, per the ship's custom, they were all counted.

☠ ☠ ☠

The pirate cannons fired as one, spitting fifteen globs of golden flame between the converging ships. Each gun had been loaded with chain shot, three cast iron balls linked by a length of chain, and the lethal rounds, aimed high, flung through the night and ripped through the *Temperance's* rigging and sails. Spars and line snapped away as the broadside's smoke lifted away on the low wind. One of the shots had crashed into the upper hull, the connected balls whipping through the bulwarks and smashing into the dark

91

human shapes aligned topside. Screams of agony and shouted orders now filled the shadowed British warship. Musket fire leapt back across the sea between them.

Swivel guns, newly positioned along the *Klymene's* rails and at her aft deck, exploded with a barrage of noise, pistol balls and scrap iron sputtering into those marines who'd rushed to the railing to fend off the expected boarding. Dubbed "murderers" by most seaman, the swivel guns made short work of the marines, their forms dancing oddly before spilling across the gangplanks. Stinkpots of sulphur were lobbed between the two ships and detonated at the British ship's center decks. Their smoke rolled across the boat, spreading on the wind and the marines moved within the haze, shouting in confusion.

One of the *Temperance's* cannons suddenly exploded, then another. The thunderous boom shook the *Klymene's* timbers, a thirty-two pounder for sure. The first ball shredded into the back top of the pirate ship's hull, gutting away wood, splinters spraying in all directions.

Then, just as suddenly as it had appeared, the *Klymene* swung away again into the cover of night. More cannon fire now erupted from the British man-o-war, its men well trained and quickly organized at the gundecks. The blast caught the retreating vessel's aft and the poop deck burst apart, chunks of its railing and floorboard flinging over the quarterdeck like a hundred cannonballs. One of the mizzenmast spars plunged towards the deck, snapping lesser spars and cables as it fell. In the darkness, screams quickly filled the back of the ship and shouts of command roared over them as the black-flagged vessel continued its escape back into the darkness from which it had just sprung.

In its wake, within the shadows between the two rolling ships, the small launch was finally secured to the side of the *Temperance*. Several men moved within the small boat as it tossed on the waves, the first already out and climbing the British hull. Just moments before, they'd shoved off as the two sterns had met, drifting dangerously between their colliding hulls, to be passed by their speed as the two vessels moved forward, falling back quickly along the *Temperance's* hull. Just forward of the rudder, several boarding axes were now hacked into that thick lumber, the boat tied off and secure until the task was done.

Roarke drove another axe into the hull, and continued his slow climb up the side of the ship. The entire craft was shaking, its cannons unloading into the night after the retreating *Klymene*. His ears hummed with their deafening bellow and the wail of the winds. He felt dizzy. The ocean winds ripped at his fingers and his arms burned and trembled as he pulled himself up to the next brace. The cold Atlantic waves splashed over his legs again, threatened to drag him into the dark water below. He was quickly passed another axe and chopped it again into the wood above his head, the uneven improvised ladder working slowly towards the dim light glowing faintly above. The ship sat heavy in the water, the gallery's cabin window already within his sight. Soon, within his reach.

In the distance, the *Klymene* had pulled ahead of the British warship as planned, leading her blindly into the night, slowing just enough so that the British would continue their fruitless chase. Very few of the man-o-war's cannons could now target her and irregular cannon fire echoed in the night.

Roarke felt the other men approaching just behind and struggled ahead. Then his hands were upon the stern gallery and he pulled himself over the ornate balustrade to the balcony. The cabin's window was flushed within with lantern light. That was encouraging. Roarke waited for the other men to complete their own climb to join him, one by one, on the gallery's small deck. Beneath them, the large ship's rudder groaned and sputtered and the black ocean rolled in caps of grey spray, where their launch and one pilot bobbed in wait.

They were five men. Five against almost two hundred. If the prisoner was not being held just within, as the light promised, he'd likely be found in the captain's quarters, and they'd have to get past those two hundred. Cannon fire rumbled again just above them and the whole platform shook.

No words were spoken as the cutlasses and dirks were drawn from their belts. No pistols. Any killing would be quiet killing. One of the men had positioned himself to kick in the door, but Roarke delayed him with his hand. Reached for the handle himself and turned it. It was unlocked, and with a nod to his men, Roarke threw the door wide open.

The pirates rushed the room as they had many boardings before. Expecting the worst, prepared to die in the next moment, blades lifted for their own killing blows, they flooded through the doorway and spread quickly across the room.

Roarke moved forward, hunched low, eyes skimming the cluttered quarters for any sign of movement. There was none. Except for the man resting comfortably in the only chair, the room proved quite empty.

The aged man appeared asleep, chin resting on his vested chest with a weather-worn copy of a book split across his broad stomach and held in place by his peacefully cupped hands. He breathed heavily, the round glasses perched at the very end of his nose quivering some with each exhale of a half-opened mouth. His hair hung loose down his neck, his large forehead glistening in the wobbling lantern light. Roarke peeked curiously at the book, *Three Comedies of Ben Jonson*, then tapped the man at his shoulder. "Mornin', sir," he tapped him again.

The man woke, eyed the room over his glasses. "Am I to gather, sir, you're the cause of all this commotion?" he said. His voice was rough and bottomless.

"Dr. Franklin?"

"That answer, young man, depends on what you plan on doing with the good doctor."

Roarke smiled. "Our intention is take him off this ship and, assuming our own is not yet at the bottom of the Atlantic, to escort him back to his United States at quickest haste with *Monsieur* Beaumarchais's warmest regards."

The older man leaned forward in the chair, caught the book in his hands. His eyes moved over the room, then looked over Roarke again. "Pirates, are you?"

"God willin'," Roarke replied.

Franklin nodded, chuckled. "Well, then, we may as well steal this book while we're at it." He handed the hardback to Roarke. "Captain Hopkins

was kind enough to lend it to me but I only got to Act Four before the hullabaloo started above," he winked. "I'm just curious, and a bit anxious, to see how Act Five unfurls, forgive the pun."

"Understood." Roarke tucked the book into the back of his belt and stepped back while Franklin fought to his feet as the ship tilted again.

Then, the British marines burst into the room.

The first two were cut down before they even realized their prisoner was no longer alone. The cutlass was a grisly weapon and its trade splashed across the doorframe, the two guards crashing to the floor amid piercing shrieks.

Red jackets flooded into the room, five more men, and calls went up the steps for more. Roarke pushed Franklin back into his chair and lunged at the closest target.

Musket fire rang out in the small room. Flame scorched Roarke's left arm, smoke now burning his eyes. A sword's blade lunged from the smoke, and he knocked it aside with his own cutlass. He felt movement behind him, saw a flash of red, and stabbed out with his dagger hand. The shape screamed and fell back into the blurred commotion.

The soldier in front of him, a man of about nineteen, he suspected, squared off and brought his sword up to parry the pirate's first feint. The boy's eyes were wide, his arm trembling. Still, he swung his blade.

Roarke caught the swing with his parrying dagger, sliding the distinctive knife down the marine's blade into the handle. The hilt broke away as expected and shattered. Roarke intentionally opened himself up to a strike, dared the marine to use the spoiled blade. The man took the bait and when their swords crashed together, the marine's hand slid up the now-exposed shaft. He screamed, several fingers sliced off at the base of his hand. The sword fell from his hand and Roarke's cutlass sank deep before the lost blade had clanged to the floor. He pulled his sword back, the body spilling to his feet, and turned to help the others.

Two of his men were down. The first lay shot and sprawled over an overturned bench, one leg twisted awkwardly over its corner. The other wriggled against the far wall at the end of a marine's sword as the soldier struggled to free the blade. Roarke screamed, charged the scene, slashed the man down. Both bodies tumbled to the floor.

He kneeled, held his hand over the spurting wound. "Merkerson, I'm sorry. We never should have — "

The pirate pushed away his captain's hand, grinned at him with teeth clenched in pain. "The mates voted, Roarke. Liberty or death, ain't that so?"

"Merkerson..." Roarke felt a hand on his shoulder, turned. Two other men were already escorting Franklin out the door.

"Captain, we've already been here too long. They'll return soon enough and in force."

"You're right." He stood and left the now-dead Merkerson on the floor. Followed the others out the gallery door to the platform, where several grappling hooks and lines waited. Over the railing, the others already had Franklin halfway down the hull. Roarke rappelled the lines easily behind them, dropped with the others down onto the waiting dinghy.

The lines were cut and tossed along the tossing waves, and the dinghy quickly fell away from the *Temperance*. The oars dug into the heaving waves.

"I am solemnly saddened for your men," Franklin said from the stern sheets, arms bundled, his round face scrunched against the ocean's spray.

Roarke pulled the book from his back, handed it to the man. "I saw his *Bartholomew Fair* once," the pirate said.

Franklin nodded.

The *Temperance* had already vanished into the night, chasing after a ship that was no longer just ahead.

Against the dark horizon, the *Klymene* now appeared beside them. Its crew crowded along the railing, many bloodied, and already bandaged from the battle. They stood defiantly, together, and above them flew the ship's updated flag.

Red with white stripes. The colonial army's colors.

"You might say I'm just curious, and a bit anxious, to see how it all turns out," Roarke muttered.

"So we shall discover together, sir. So we shall together." Franklin had leaned forward to pat Roarke's knee.

"God willin'," the pirate said.

NOTES: *When the colonies declared independence in 1776, the Continental Navy had only thirty ships to contest a British armada of just under three hundred warships. By issuing "Letters of Marque" to armed merchant ships, and known pirates, the colonial navy instantly added 1,500 ships and 15,000 guns to its fleet. By 1777, when Washington's army totaled about 11,000 men, another 11,000 were privateers at sea intercepting British shipping in the Atlantic and Caribbean. These men alone cost the King some 2,000 British ships, £18 million, and the capture of 12,000 men.*

Pierre Beaumarchais was a French inventor, musician, politician, publisher, and spy, but is best known for his dramatic works The Barber of Séville *and* The Marriage of Figaro. *During the early years of the American Revolution, Beaumarchais worked with Franklin and others as a French agent charged with recruiting privateers and smuggling arms and supplies to the colonials prior to France's official alliance. His deliveries particularly helped win the battle of Saratoga, a key victory that made it easier for France to enter an alliance with the United States, which Franklin successfully gained in 1778. Though Franklin's ship to France was pursued by English cruisers several times during the long voyage, there is no official record that he was ever captured.*

Long before the American or French revolutions, pirate crews were indeed remarkably democratic. The captain of each ship was typically determined by vote and he could be replaced by another vote at any time if the crew so wished. Even the choice of which ships to attack or which ports to head for were regularly put to a general vote. The captain assumed absolute rule only when the ship was in battle.

THE SHO'MEN

1817, MARYLAND

They thought they'd picked the perfect spot to bury the treasure. Halfway up the Chester River, two miles northeast from the small port, and atop the highest hill. The coins and jewels were carefully stacked in a small oak chest, which was then wrapped in a worn sail and buried five feet deep, crowned with a dark slab of local fieldstone they'd found. When the time came, it would be a simple matter of digging it all back up again.

But almost twenty years had passed before they'd returned, so, though the treasure was exactly where they'd left it, some damned fool had gone and built a college over it.

"A simple matter of burnin' it to the ground," offered Foster, capping a string of profanity which had lasted almost a full half hour.

"We can't do that."

"Why the 'ell not?" Foster replied.

The second pirate shrugged, unsure of a significant answer, so the last man, by looks younger than the other two by some thirty years, spoke for him. "Maybe a touch extreme, is all. Surely there's another way."

They studied the building again: a tall four-story brick with an attic and two attached wings, four dozen windows, and a pair of doors. Several of the windows were missing panes and only one of the doors had steps, a wide plank laid from the ground up to the other doorway. Smoke drifted away on a cool Chesapeake breeze from a single chimney on the eastern face of the school.

William, the younger man who'd spoken, shook off the wind's chill. The act evoked dim memories of the first and last time he'd been here, when their three shadowed forms worked through the night until the crimson glow of dawn. He'd been only eight then, a gaunt and crafty cabin boy working aboard the *Pandora*, flagship of the infamous Captain Cataldo. Foster and Sweeney had crewed the same and though William had grown tall and square shouldered over the years, with a man's sharp chin and arms and eyes hardened by the brutal work at sea, the older men remained almost the same as the night they'd buried stolen treasure together. A bit heavier for sure, and greyer too, the stubble of their beards now peppered with white. But mostly the same.

"We get inside that building," Foster said. "And we break that bloody floor open."

Sweeney groaned. "And dig."

"Aye," Foster said rubbing his lower back and eyeing the younger man, "And then bloody dig"

"Without the rock, we won't know the exact spot. It could take weeks."

"Ain't it worth it, Sweeney?"

William watched Sweeney as he imagined the treasure and coins they'd hidden together. Sweeney groaned again. "It is."

"Then it takes weeks."

"And all the people?" William reminded.

"We kill 'em."

"Can't do that."

"Why the 'ell not? Fine." Foster waved off the argument, "Then take 'em as 'ostages?"

"Too long." Sweeney took off the top hat he'd recently stolen and scratched his balding head. "We'll be weeks diggin', mate. Someone would come lookin' for 'em."

"Then," Foster glared, "Wot you're tellin' me is the only way to get our deserved treasures is by movin' about that miserable college for weeks without anyone wonderin' what three motley seadogs such as we be really doin'."

"In short."

Foster shook his head, chewed his tongue in thought with the few teeth he had, his eyes going back and forth between the building and his two conspirators. "Fine," he said at last. "Then 'tis time to cut away the anchors, mates."

"What's that mean?" asked William.

"It means wash your face, boy," said Foster. "You're bloody going to college."

Mr. Stack, the school's principal, sat behind a worn desk in a small room watched over by a portrait of George Washington, the painting having provided the last five minutes of his customary pitch. The two men, a father and son by introduction, sat across from him with forced smiles and newly-shaven faces.

"In short," Stack concluded for them, "The college bears his name not so much for his generous donation, but for the noble pathways he demonstrated to the young men of this country. Fifty-six of those same men now attend this institution for a proper classical education in composition, logic, philosophy, and the higher branches of arithmetic. Students at Washington College come to know men such as Horace, Homer, and Virgil."

"They the teachers here, then?"

"Precisely, Mr. Plank," Stack beamed. "I see you're a man who understands my meaning and the worth of a classical education."

"Indeed I is, mate, indeed I is. What time does 'e start?"

"August, naturally. William would matriculate with next term's First Year class and —"

"No, no. What time *tomorrow*, I mean."

"Sir, that's really quite impossible." Stack frowned, stopped himself, then tried again. "This year is already almost halfway over and he'd be —"

The pouch of coins landed heavily at the center of the principal's table.

"What time tomorrow?"

Stack avoided looking directly at the bag. "Your son would be at a tremendous disadvantage, sir. We haven't even truly discussed his previous schooling yet. The school in San Juan, William, how far did you get in your Latin studies?"

"Mostly spoke Spanish, sir," the young man replied. "Learned a bit of French from a girl in Guadeloupe once who — "

"Lad's a talent with languages, 'e is." The older man kneed the boy's chair. "Weren't no problem there."

Stack studied the two. Their shoes and pants were shabby, and only their jackets looked new, so much so, he thought with a smile, one might think they'd been bought just minutes before the interview. Traders from Puerto Rico, apparently. An import business of sorts, the father had bragged. Just off the ship.

"The First Years also study algebra," he told them, still not sure what to make of the pair. "Euclid's *Elements*, the *Aeneid*, Greek grammar, the *Graeca Minora*, the *Commentaries of Caesar* —"

"Sounds sportin' it does. 'E'll start tomorrow, yes?"

Stack sighed. "Tuition is twenty dollars, sir. Boarders pay a hundred."

"'E's a boarder for sure, Mr. Stack. In fact," the older man added, nodding towards the pouch between them, "I'll likely be about the grounds meself a bit. Just to make sure the lad's fittin' in and keepin' to the books."

"I'm not sure the other students would —"

"Well," the man smiled. "I'd be more than 'appy to talk with them personally on that matter, Mr. Stack."

"That would be quite unnecessary, sir!" Stack stood to lead them from the room and scooped up the pouch, holding it out to the older man. "I fear I've spoken in haste. Perhaps I should first discuss the matter with the school board at the earliest —"

"Principal Stack," Both men stood with him, the older pushing back the money. "We're lookin' to settle in Rock Hall, I think."

"The Eastern Shore's a fine place to settle, sir."

"Indeed. I've strived me 'ole life, workin' an honest man's day as a man of ships, so this 'ere lad could get a proper education. There be a new world in those books, see, and I think he should see that world awhile. On me own mother, I swear there ain't another school on Earth I'd rather see him go."

"You're very kind," Mr. Stack laughed, very much relieved. "And also a very persuasive man, Mr. Plank."

"You 'ave no idea."

The principal blinked, smiled clumsily, replaying the dark gleam that had just crossed the man's eyes. "Well then," he managed, shaking off the look and turning to William. "I suppose it's welcome to Washington College."

"Thank you, sir."

☠ ☠ ☠

The college, it turned out, had a basement. At first, the discovery merely brought more violent cursing and a second proposal to burn down the school, the assumption being that the treasure had surely already been found when the foundation was laid. Another look, however, proved the basement was more of a cellar that ran only beneath part of the building and that, from their combined estimates and recollection, the prize was buried under the left wing of the school and had yet not been disturbed. The option, then, became either to dig straight down through the floor of Mr. Gillin's classroom, hoping the instructor or his students would not notice the growing hole in their floor each morning and the three men crowded about it, or to break through the basement wall and tunnel *sideways* towards their purpose. They hacked through the wall that same night.

They worked in the dark cellar, digging through the day and night and discarding the dirt after the students had gone to sleep, a hooded lantern cast over the narrow opening throughout, the hole easily covered with a stack of boxes. Only twice had Jefferson, the Negro caretaker, come down for some garden tools. It had been two weeks already and the tunnel was now long enough and wide enough that Sweeney napped comfortably within during one of their breaks.

Just beneath, William lay sprawled on his stomach beside the lantern. Two books lay opened on the floor, and his fingers moved quickly between them. "And, once again the r...rav'nous harpies return," the whispered translations drifted up to Sweeney. "Or from the — the — the dark recesses where they lie."

"What's a harpy?" the older pirate asked.

William marked his spot with his finger and rolled to a sitting position. "From what I can gather, they seem to be nude women with wings, hideous faces, and sharp nails, who like to kill sailors."

"Sounds like Barbados," the older man mused, "'cepting the wings, course. 'Tis a sea tale, then?"

"It is, actually." He turned the book in his hands. "A captain called Aeneas and his mates trying to get home after a God-cursed wind pushes 'em off course. Sea monsters, foreign queens. He even goes into Hell."

"As all fittin' capt'ns do, lad. As they all do."

William laughed. "No, it's just to visit. They sail out again."

"Just to visit?" The other pirate whistled. "Who'd imagine such a thing?"

William turned the book in his hands. "Virgil did," he replied quietly.

As he spoke, the basement door opened and Foster's dark form worked slowly down the steps towards them. "Grab yer shovels, mates," he whispered, blowing the cold from his fingers, "We're close as sin, we are. I just know it."

"William," Sweeney nodded. "Why don't ye tell Foster one of those Captain Aeneas yarns."

"Who's 'e?" said Foster, grabbing a bucket. "'E that Aruban wot got 'is legs bit off?"

William laughed and climbed into the hole to help Sweeney scoop away the dirt. "Well, how 'bout when they meet Charybdis. She's a sea monster that looks just like a giant whirlpool, but used to be a beautiful sea nymph."

Sweeney turned with a big grin. "Sounds like a good one, lad." So William started the tale, and the digging began again.

☠ ☠ ☠

Lured by an unusually warm January afternoon, a half dozen students had gathered beneath the college's large elm tree, one of the more popular spots for after-class studies and gossip. Though any passerby looking casually at the group of young men would have assumed William was merely another among them, a closer study would have revealed that he remained, literarily and symbolically, just outside the immediate ring. It was not a spot he was unaccustomed to.

Growing up at sea, starting as a cabin boy aboard the privateer ship *Conquerant*, he'd spent the bulk of his life tracking safely just outside the main circle. The crews were largely made of brutal and violent men who on occasion killed only for sport. He'd quickly learned to remain close enough to always discover something new, but never so close that he'd become one of them. Whether that was his choice or theirs, he was not yet sure.

And, though the young men of Washington College swore far less and carried no pistols, William had carefully applied the same logic. He knew for certain he was not one of them and so sat just close to see what he might learn of Euclid, Cicero, and Caesar.

This day, however, the students' heated discussion was not on the problems of the world's classics, but rather, on one of the world's most classic problems.

"How shall I convince her to say yes?"

The boy who spoke was named Thomas, a stout blond-haired fellow whose father owned a corn plantation near Salisbury. He was one of the better students, William knew, and also one of those the others most admired.

"How shall *you*?" laughed another. "How shall I? For I am much closer to the prize. She and I have spoken twice already, my good Mr. Taylor."

"A passing 'good afternoon' on High street, perhaps? I thought as much. Well," Thomas laughed. "Have faith, Mr. Lynch. Rome was not built in a day."

"Epictetus?"

"Ovid, obviously. The *Metamorphoses*."

"Yes, of course."

"The Kent Ball is next week, gentlemen. Perhaps we should seek other ball dates among the rest of the women's college." But the subject of the prized female would not be dropped.

"My brother wrote and suggested I arrange for a delivery of flowers."

"I know a girl at the school who is friends with her," added another. "And she is to bring me up in a favorable light."

"Alas, men," one chuckled, "I fear the gifted Miss Coulter is not one to spend time among mortals such as we."

"Have any of you even asked her yet?" A voice suddenly spoke above the rest and the other students turned to look. Several had puzzled expressions and even William, himself, had been surprised to hear the sound of his own voice.

"What was that?" Thomas asked for them.

"Well, has anyone asked her?" William lowered his book. "It's difficult for a girl to say yes unless you go ahead and actually ask her."

Several of the other boys laughed, nudging the first.

"Our would-be sho'man speaks. I'd always assumed your Caribbean girls only needed a few coins. Mr. Plank, is it? But no, 'ask them' he says."

"William, please. And, yes. You look a girl in the eye and tell her what you really want and why. That's that. Whether in Havana, Southampton or Charlestown. I have found the matter both undemanding and rewarding."

"A dangerous combination." Thomas nodded.

"Indeed."

"And are you willing to wager, *William*, twenty dollars on said matter?" The students around Thomas whistled and groaned. The stake was significant. "Assuming you have as much," grinned the boy, purposely examining William's clothing.

"Oh," William smiled back, "I'll manage to dig it up somewhere."

☠ ☠ ☠

Later, William sneaked into the cellar to work beside the others. Now, five weeks into the dig, the hole beneath the school twisted and split like a stunted rabbit burrow. Still, there was no sign of the chest. Foster had stopped promising that they were close two weeks before.

"Sorry I'm late," William said, moving into the dim lantern light. "Got held up. You two take a break. I'll dig more than my fair share again tonight."

"You need to sleep, lad," Sweeney said.

"A good floggin's all he needs," Foster grunted. "He's always late anymore."

"That a new book?" Sweeney had crawled out of the hole.

"Begad! Enough with the black-spotted books. We've got diggin' to do, or 'as the lad now properly forgotten why we *really* be 'ere?"

"Gangway! I'll dig, I'll dig," William grabbed the small spade from Foster's hand. "It's Caesar," he told Sweeney, handing over the book as he crawled into the tunnel. "His account of the Gallic war and his civil wars with Pompey. It's quite remarkable, really. I marked a few pages I thought you'd like that I'll read at break."

"No breaks, ye scurvy swab. And, unless 'e's carrying a bloody shovel, there'll be no Caesar 'ere tonight either."

William laughed as he started digging. "Foster, did you know the great Caesar was once captured and ransomed by pirates? A brutal crew who sailed the Mediterranean sea. Held him for months."

"Ha!" Foster tapped the dagger at his hip. "Now that's a tale worth hearin', lad."

"Of, course," William nudged Sweeney, "After he was released, Caesar returned with twenty Roman ships and crucified the lot of them. Just as he'd always told them he would while they reckoned he was joking."

Foster's eyes narrowed in the shadows into shining black gems. "Dig, bucko."

William and Sweeney laughed and moved further back into the tunnel. "So, where were you?" the older pirate asked.

"Had to talk to some lass named Coulter down at the girls' college." William shook his head. "Apparently she and I are going to some dance next week."

The professor returned his paper, a quiz on the fifth chapter of Euclid's *Elements* with a *D* emblazoned at its bottom left corner. William spent the remainder of the class staring absently out the room's window, thinking. He didn't even realize when the class had ended or that several students were now crowded around his desk.

"William," the boy named Campbell said. "I, well, I would like your opinion on something."

William turned slowly towards them, slid his quiz out of their view. "Sure," he said slowly, looking at the others.

"Having some trouble with a few of the local men."

For the first time, William noticed that Campbell was sporting a wide bruise on the right side of his face. He knew what kind of trouble he spoke of.

"Couple of dock guys," Thomas confirmed. "Caught him on Queen the other night. Roughed him up some, took all his money."

"'Tis a rough street. Best to be avoided." William shook his head. "Let that be the end of it."

"No," Campbell said. "That's just the thing. It's not the end of it. I work part time at a shop on High and Cross and they said, they said if they saw me again, I was to pay two dollars. Each time."

William paused. "And what do you think about that?"

"I think, well," he looked him in the eye. "I think I'd rather die first."

"That's a start," William smiled. "Once you've got that decided, the rest is easy."

"So, what would you do?" Thomas asked.

"How many?"

"Four," Campbell said. "There were four. Seen 'em before."

"Figured out who their captain is?"

"The one talking, I assume."

"Usually," William nodded. "Next time you meet, right away break his nose. When he goes down, keep kickin' no matter what the others do. You should have back up. And make sure you're wearing heavy boots." He nodded with satisfaction. "That's what I'd do."

"Heavens," one of the other students grunted. "Seems a little extreme, doesn't it?"

William shrugged. "I've seen men pelted with broken bottles. Frayed line stuffed in their mouths and lit afire. Captain Cataldo once sewed a man's lips shut because he'd teasingly mentioned mutiny. *Deos fortioribus adesse.* Tacitus, yes?"

"The gods are on the side of the strong," Thomas translated, grinning.

Campbell shook his head. "Right. I'll do what you say," he said, his eyes burning with purpose. "A bit of danger sounds tempting, actually. But I wouldn't know the first thing about breaking someone's nose. Could you —Would you —"

"Teach you to break a man's nose."

"Yes." Several of the others were nodding their heads also.

William studied the small circle. "And will you mates show me how to find the greatest common measure of two given numbers not relatively prime?"

"Oh," Thomas said, "Euclid just uses his *antenaresis* notion again in that proposition. Only a matter of repeatedly subtracting the smaller number. It's simple, really."

"As simple as breaking a man's nose, no doubt," William said.

Principal Stack sighed, his hands folded neatly across the top of his desk. William and Foster sat just across from him, awaiting the next words. "I simply have no choice in the matter, Mr. Plank," he continued. "Our regulations are very clear."

"But it was only an innocent scuffle," Foster argued.

"Your son beat two men unconscious," Stack hollered back, "and with one of the victim's own boots no less."

"He'd pulled a knife on Campbell, sir. I couldn't —"

"While I do admire the defense of your classmate, William, it is, re-gardless, a situation you two never should have been in. Campbell shattered the man's nose so badly, the poor soul almost choked to death on his own blood."

"Yes, sir." William struggled to suppress his smile.

"Your instructors report you're a promising student, William. Lacking in fundamentals, by all accounts, but quite superb in your thoughts and academic curiosity. I have no desire to expel you. Instead, you and Mr. Campbell are to be fined five dollars each and will serve a month-long probation, in which you will remain in your rooms or the library when not in class."

"'Is room, begad! Are you insane, man? Do ye 'ave any idea how close we must —"

"After, I hope, your son will have a greater respect for our rules and expectations."

"Oh, blast it to 'ell,' Foster raged. "I 'ave an idea, Mr. Stack." He fumbled for the pouch of coins in his jacket.

Principal Stack waved both hands violently. "No, Mr. Plank. That is not a solution to this matter. Five dollars is the full extent of the fine."

"Are you certain, Stack? The lad tells me you're starting a lottery of some kind to raise money for the school. This would be a fittin' start."

"Entirely not, sir."

Foster shrugged. "It could have been." He stood from his chair, his hand dangerously close, noticed William, to the dagger on his hip, a long stiletto. "There are other options, or course."

"Foster!" William reached out a hand to stop him. "No."

"Leave us, lad," the pirate snarled, staring only at the principal. "Mr. Stack and I be needin' to discuss this matter of probation."

"Don't," William said. "Please. It's just not the way things are done here."

"It's all right, William," Mr. Stack said with confident assurance just behind him. "You may return to your room now. Your father and I will then finish this discussion as civilized men."

Just before the fire started, and after seven weeks of digging, they found the chest.

Its wood and canvas were rotted, broken away immediately, and the coins and jewels spilled onto Sweeney's head just like Boston hailstones. The treasure was collected and placed in three small bags. Enough for each to return to any of the Leeward Islands a rich man.

The streets of Chestertown would likely prove mostly empty, they knew, and they would move quickly past the High Street shops and taverns and to the waterfront without particular notice. And, just past the docks, along the tall brown undergrowth across from Water Street waited their boat, a twenty-foot fishing boat they'd stolen months before. It was a simple matter now of working down the Chester and picking up passage in Cambridge.

"Is the boat ready?" Foster gasped, the three shapes trundling in the darkness down the hill and away from the school in much the same way they'd sneaked up so many years before.

"It's been arranged," William said. "By the way, what did you say to Principal Stack?"

Foster cleared his throat. "Whate'er do ye mean? We just spoke as men, is all."

"He's resigned. Won't be back next term."

"A shame, it 'tis. He's a noble man of learnin', 'e is."

A shadowed form stepped suddenly from the darkness.

"Avast, ye rat!" Foster held the others back, and drew his pistol.

"Wait," William squeezed his arm. "He's with me."

"William!" The figure moved forward slowly, dressed in the somber colors of the age. "Thomas and some of the others were lookin' for you," Campbell told William. "They suspect something."

"We'd best keep movin' then."

"Who the 'ell is 'e?" asked Foster.

"Campbell," William explained, shaking the boy's hand. "The one that broke the fellow's nose."

"Pleased to meet ye Campbell. Ye sound like a first-rate lad." He'd rebelted his pistol. "But, we 'ave a pressing engagement."

"I know. The boat's ready"

"What do ye mean?" Foster glared. "William, lad. What have ye done?"

Before he could explain, William noticed that Campbell was looking past them both, his face strangely tilted. "My God," the boy pointed behind them. "The college."

The college. Up the hill, a strange glow spread from the bottom of the school. Just like a sunrise, blood red and treasure gold. The building was on fire.

"Damn you," William lunged at Foster, but Sweeney stepped quickly between them. "How could you?"

"It wasn't me, lad." Foster watched the peculiar glistening light flicker down the hill towards them. "I swear on me own mother." William still fought towards him. "Very well," he stammered, "On me treasure, then, I swear on me share of the prize. I 'ad nothing to do with this."

Campbell shook his head, his eyes wide. "What if it was the men from Queen Street. What have I done?"

"I need to go back," William gasped as Sweeney released him. "They'll need help."

"No," Foster grabbed his arm. "There ain't time, lad. Even if they get it put out, they'll find our work below. Too many questions. We need to cut anchor."

"You three go. I'm staying anyway."

"Staying," Sweeney understood first. "You three?"

"I'm staying with the college. I have enough money now to — Well, I've decided to stay on a bit."

"But ye can't, lad." Foster's face has scrunched in confusion, in hurt. "We need ye. If only to row the bloody boat."

William laughed. "Look, Campbell can help get you far as Cambridge. Perhaps further, if you agree." The other boy nodded and William handed him a small pouch of coins. Foster noticed for the first time that Campbell carried a bag.

"I should very much like to see the Caribbean for a time, sir," the boy said to him, very much like William might have, but in a softer way.

"And he breaks a fine nose, I hear." Sweeney patted the boy's shoulder and moved to William. "You'll write, surely. Tell me more of them stories?"

"I promise."

The huge man squeezed him in his arms and William laughed at the grip.

"That it, then," Foster said behind them. "You just go your own way."

"For awhile, captain. I'll see you all again soon enough." William's eyes were already focused on the fire above, the bodies moving up the hill towards it. He started after them, then stopped and turned back. "You once told the principal there was a new world in those books," he said. "And that I should see that world awhile."

"Aye, lad. I did." Foster looked stiff in the darkness. His face was a mask of emotions.

"There's more treasure to be found up that hill," William said, and started to run.

The grey-haired pirate nodded, watched the boy go. "And you'll surely find it," he said.

NOTES: *The Chesapeake Bay, with its countless creeks and coves, proved an ideal destination for pirate captains and their crews to come in from the Atlantic and hide ships and captured prizes. Roger Makeele, Stede Bonnet, and Joseph Wheland are all notorious for stashing prizes along Maryland's Eastern Shore, and pirate-age treasure has been recovered from Caroline County to Salisbury. Washington College, the tenth oldest college in the nation, was founded in 1780 in part with money bestowed by George Washington, who remained on the college's Board of Visitors and Governors until he became the country's first President. In December of 1817, the school indeed mysteriously caught fire and Mr. Stack, the college's principal, indeed resigned unexpectedly. Prizes were awarded by the school board to students Thomas Taylor and James Lynch for acts of bravery during the fire. The building was rebuilt the following year following a peculiarly successful student-run lottery. Today, the college is home to some 1,400 students seeking a liberal arts and sciences education in more than thirty subjects. The school's athletic teams are nicknamed the Sho'men, an enduring moniker that goes back to pre-colonial times and is bestowed to those who've made their life on the Eastern Shore.*

DAYBREAK BOYS

1848, NEW YORK

The two boys departed the tenement building and proceeded down Murderer's Alley together. The notorious path was narrow, only three feet wide between the two buildings, and they walked single file, stepping over several shadowed forms.

The boy in front was shorter, gaunt with bulging eyes and thin ashen hair, his face almost skeletal in the early evening light as he scurried past the others. His companion, flat-faced with a badly broken nose and dead eyes that stayed half closed no matter the time of day, loped slowly behind, his broad shoulders hunched over with experience. Both boys were fifteen.

The Old Brewery, their only home for all these long years, loomed over them as they crossed the congested street. This dead thing of the Five Corners, the brewery squatted five stories high over the quarter's other apartments, saloons, and dance halls, its yellow skin peeling and pocked like some leprous corpse. Inside, a thousand souls persistently fueled its wafting stench and its ever-present drone of lamentation. And as always, the punched-black eyes of its shattered windows watched the boys as they crept out from its shadow. They turned the corner and kept walking.

Neither had ever been this far from the Old Brewery. Never more than a block since the day they'd been born, which, in and of itself, was more wandering than many. Some had never left the building, even once, in all their years on Earth, and others just stood in its doorways, as afraid of going out into the streets as the public was at the notion of ever going *in*.

Twice, the smaller boy turned to persuade the other forward. "Don't you want to be a pirate?" he asked him, and the other shrugged.

By now they'd crossed Mulberry Street and stood at the center of Paradise Square. More dance houses and taverns lined each corner and a swarm of people moved between them: men in stovepipe hats, chewing on tobacco and looking for a worthwhile fight, women carrying bundles, children, and bottles of gin. Raucous music and drunken laughter drifted from the doorways. The air was fresher here, the reek of the Old Brewery lost to new scents of the pubs and an open sewer that ran towards the river. The remnants of a small park, nothing now but mud and filth-choked trees, still cowered in the middle of the Square behind a ramshackle fence. The smaller boy eyed some of the drying clothing which lined the entire length of the fence, but several younger boys armed with brickbats and clubs guarded the palings.

The boy smiled and turned the other away. In the distance, the dreadful silhouette of The Tombs loomed on the dark horizon. The building's black shape soared toward the night sky, stark and cruel. Saul could imagine its hundred gallows lined across the yard within. He'd been told once the jailhouse's design was copied from an ancient Egyptian burial chamber and he studied it awhile with some appreciation for its honesty. Brick for brick and line for line, it was, like its forebear, a building formed for death.

The crowd bustling past them looked poor, a swirling hodgepodge of intoxicated sailors, oystermen, laborers, and low-salaried clerks. No one with real money would dare come into the Square, or down in the Five Points. A man like that would be gutted and left naked in some back alley in a wink. In the Old Brewery, he'd seen a little girl murdered for a penny she'd begged. Her body had lain in the corner of the room for five days. Only the penniless dared roam the Five Points. The real money was elsewhere. The boys kept walking.

They followed the open sewer, the thin trail leading away from the crowded Five Points. The crowd was remained thick and several young men purposely slammed into the boys as they passed, looking for an excuse to fight or touching them for any coin.

"Hot corn! Hot corn! Here's your lily white corn!" A soprano call suddenly rose over the crowd's mumbling.

Saul stopped to watch her. She was no more than fourteen herself, and carried a cedar-staved bucket in the hollow of her fair-skinned arm. She wore no shoes, but was dressed in spotted calico with wavy dark hair that hung long and free over her plaid shawl. The lamplight she stood beneath gave her entire face a pleasing glow. She shined just like gold.

"Hey, look at that," he grabbed his friend. "Right there. Ain't she the prettiest damn thing you ever seen in your whole rotten life?" His companion shrugged.

"Hot corn! Come buy my lily white corn." She stopped, noticed him looking at her. "Hot corn!"

Inside the basket were a dozen piping ears. The boy wiped his mouth with the back of his hand. It had been three days since his last meal.

"Love, you got any money?" she asked, studying him.

He shook his head.

"Hot corn!" She shouted again, turning back towards the crowd. "All you that's got money. Poor me that's got none!"

"What's your name," he asked behind her.

"Molly," she said, shifting the weight of the basket.

He watched the hair swish over her shoulders. "That's a pretty name."

"Sure. Look, love. I got work to do."

"Sure, sure. Hey —"

"What is it?"

"I'll have money next time."

"Great."

"Lots of money."

"Sure, love."

He smiled. "Hey, Molly, which way to Water Street?"

"Just keep going that way," she nodded. "Past Cherry."

He watched her vanish into the crowd, her cries of "hot corn" lifting again into the night. *The prettiest damn thing*, he thought again to himself. *Just like gold.* Then he started moving again.

They'd entered the Fourth Ward, moving down Cherry Street. He'd heard the area was once where New York's aristocrats and wealthy merchants had lived, but saw no sign of that now. Here, more filthy tenements lined each street, and every other one advertised a saloon or house of prostitution amid its basement or upper floors. The road overflowed with rubbish, vomit, and human feces. Several children sat beside the road and threw stones at a three-legged dog. Grimy bodies pressed past each other violently in the darkness, the gang colors obvious at every turn. For here were the dives that sheltered the infamous river pirates: the Buckoos and Swamp Angels, the Short Tails and the Patsy Conroys. And, of course, one more. The gang the two boys had come to see.

On Water Street at last, running parallel with what could only be the East River, they found the house. The low gin mill at Slaughter House Point, at the intersection of James Street. Half a dozen young men lingered outside the front stoop and muscled to attention as the boys approached.

"You come for a beatin', Five Pointer pig?"

The larger boy stepped forward, as if to welcome the offer, but the first held him back and tossed the blade he carried to the one who'd spoken.

The sharp-faced man, no more than twenty, with striped trousers stuck in his boots, scowled at the knife as the rest of the gang circled around them. "What's this, muppet?"

"Give it to McCarthy."

"McCarthy, he says." He smirked rotten teeth at the others, turned the blade over. "Back in a minute, men. You can kill 'em if you want." He disappeared through the doorway into the darkness of the mill. The two boys waited quietly, surrounded by the others, who'd now drawn nailed clubs and short butcher knives, flexing and muttering behind them.

The first thug returned, signaling the others away. "Let's go, pigs."

They were led down steps thru a dark saloon with a sand-strewn floor and a dozen dark shapes lumped at several tables. Three young men, sailors from their dress, leaned against the bar, one sucking from one of the liquor hoses. They moved down a narrow passage and filed down a series of steps to a back door. Their guide knocked twice, then stepped inside and waved them in.

In the back room, half a dozen young men sat around a table. Two had their feet up and were drinking ale. One, a giant man of perhaps twenty with short red hair and a thick mustache, stood guard at the door. The last two worked at the lock of a small chest, which lay on the table. The floor was stacked with shadowed and tarp-covered crates and barrels.

One of those working at the chest, a dark-featured teen with a hard face marked in deep scars, nodded to the knife on the table. "Where'd you find it?" he asked, still picking at the lock.

"The Old Brewery."

The room cast confirming glances.

"Belonged to a friend of ours."

"I know. He was killed," Saul said.

"You the two who done it?"

"No. But we know who did."

The scarred teen looked up from the chest. "And you'll help us find them."

"Yes."

"I'm McCarthy."

"Saul. He's Howlett."

"How'd you two know to come here?"

The red-haired giant had moved in closer behind them.

"Your man, Perris was his name, right? They took their time on him, see." One of the others had drawn a pistol as Saul spoke, his eyes burning with fury in the dim room. "He talked a lot then. About the Daybreak Boys and the Slaughter House on Water Street."

"That miserable worm! I always knew Perris was a worthless knob."

"He also said something about —" he automatically eyed the chest on the table. "— Something about the treasure. The treasure he'd get 'em if they him left alive."

"Damn him again. And you two just stood there, I suppose."

"What would you have done?"

119

McCarthy nodded. "Anything else, Five Pointer?"

"We came to join the Daybreak Boys. We want to be river pirates."

One of the shadowed figures behind McCarthy laughed.

"Pirates, eh? They want to be pirates now." He looked around the room. "This ain't no place for no Five Pointers, boy. Only reason you're still alive is because two ain't enough and you're gonna help us find more. Perris was a rat, but he was our rat, see? We'll burn down the bloody building. This is the Water Front, *boyo*. Death's thirst ain't never quenched down here."

"We came to join the Daybreak Boys."

McCarthy grabbed the knife. "And what do you think you could do for us?"

"Your booty from last night, Captain," he said, pointing to the chest. "Me father was a wretched dog but a noted screwsman in 'is day. Showed me a bit of the trade. I'd pick that lock for starts."

The scar-faced man stroked his thin mustache.

"And Howlett," Saul continued. "Well, Howlett's a natural bruiser, he is."

"Is that so?" McCarthy looked around the room. "How 'bout we show these Fivers what a bruiser on the wharfs is, men. I'm starting to think we can find the ones that killed Perris without your help. Maybe we could —"

CRACKKK!

Someone screamed, a horrible sound, and the red-haired sentry fell to his knees, gripping his hand. Two of his fingers dangled limply over the grip, jagged bone peaking though the skin, snapped off at the lowest knuckle.

"What the devil!" McCarthy screamed angrily and the others jumped from their chairs.

The giant writhed on the floor and his wails now filled the small room as several more gang members swiftly emerged through a hidden doorway, pistols and knives drawn. Through it all, Howlett remained standing sleepily over the wounded man. He was smiling.

"Well then," Saul said, looking about the room, "How about I take a look at that treasure chest."

Molly wore the new dress he'd bought her and looked as beautiful as ever while they sat together in the upper benches and watched the grey terrier gnash the giant wharf rats.

The crowd around them, close to a hundred men and a few dozen women, cheered and gabbed, seated in tiered rows around the wide sand-bottomed ring in the center of the room. Within, the dog sped about the blood-spattered pit, chomping down on the dozen remaining black forms as they scampered about, shaking each catch before tossing it aside and moving to the next. The room stunk of animal, ale, and musty sweat.

"He's a fine dog," Nicholas Saul leaned towards her. "Makes good and sure their backs is broken before he moves on." Molly smiled thinly and took a bite from the steamed yam he'd bought her. "Scrawny things, though," Saul added quickly, adjusting his new stovepipe hat. "Compared to wot we saw in the Brewery. The rats was bigger than the dogs down there, luv." She looked at him with cool eyes, and he rushed on. "Once saw one snatch a two-year-old, I did. Dragged him into one of them dirty holes. Big as the dog himself, that one was. Never saw the lad again." He lifted a hand to order two more ales.

Time was called amid cheers and the bloodied dog led away, the dead rats collected into a basket for future sausages and meat pies while bet payouts were made throughout the lantern-lit room. Saul paid for the ale and passed one to Molly. "How about tomorrow night?" he said. "I could take you to a dance hall, perhaps, if I might. I mean, if you wouldn't mind very much."

"Maybe, love," she smiled and drank from the tin cup. "Lots of corn to sell, you know."

"Sure, sure." He scratched at his ear. "Maybe I could buy it all again. Then we might go."

"You don't have to do that, dear," she said, looking about the room. "That'd be neat. Hey, ain't that your pirate pals?"

Saul looked up and followed her gaze to the front of the room where several shadowed forms stared back. The Daybreak Boys. He saw Slobbery

Jim and Patsy the Barber. Bill Johnson too. And Howlett stood with them. Sow Madden, a fifth who'd appeared in the crowd, waved Saul over.

"So late already," he said. "Best get going."

"What you gonna rob tonight?" she asked. "Think you'll find the cash box again? Real pirates, huh? There might even be a gun battle, I bet. Just like in the stories."

"Hey," he said and reached into his pocket, fishing out the last coins. Below, another dog, a tan beefy bitch, was being led to the pit. "Take this, hey. Down payment on that corn for tomorrow night."

"Thanks, love," she smiled, her face shining like the sun. "You're a real special guy."

Saul felt his own face flush, bowed quickly, and scooted past the other spectators. The Daybreak Boys waited just outside.

☠ ☠ ☠

Blanketed in darkness, they moved the boats swiftly down the East River towards the docked merchant ships. The Boys' fleet consisted of two small rowboats that they kept hidden in the sewers found under the Dover Street bridge. Saul was used to such places. The Old Brewery had been full of secret tunnels and lower levels built into the sewer system and gutters. He, like the others, was born to the stench and the rats. At dawn, when the watchmen had grown groggy or fallen asleep completely, when the crew was still ashore passed out on a night's drink or finally napping in one of the illicit houses, the river pirates would be in position to strike again.

The oars were muffled, wrapped in cloth, so the boats made almost no sound at all as the boys reached the docks. They gave a wide berth to the first two piers which had gas lights and a watchman at each. Beyond, a dozen boats were moored along the dockyard, another twenty anchored in the open river to avoid any trouble along the wharfs. Several had bodies huddled in darkness on watch. "Well then," McCarthy whispered, "Which is it tonight, Fiver."

Saul looked over the various ships. He'd established a reputation with McCarthy for having a bit of luck in knowing which were the worthwhile boardings. The red-colored tint of dawn spilled across the dark water between the ships as his eyes moved over each shadowed vessel, considering, as the others had taught him, each shape and name, port of origin, how low each rested in the water, the number of watchmen posted, if any. Found one —

"The sloop," he decided, pointing. "Philadelphia."

McCarthy and the others eyed the ship. "One guard."

"Right. One very nervous guard." Saul's fingers traced the watchman's shadowed form pacing back and forth along the ship's deck. "While the rest of 'em sleep and drink the night away." Saul turned to his captain. "This one expects to be robbed tonight. Thinks he's been put in charge of something worth stealing."

"Well then," McCarthy grinned. "We daren't disappoint the bloke." He waved the second boat closer. "Barber, take your boys and get around him at the stern. Make it shoddy enough that he's lookin' your way to see who's makin' all the noise, but not enough to wake up the whole bloody river."

"Got it."

While Patsy the Barber took his crew towards the front of the intended ship, McCarthy steered the other rowboat past several ships and then doubled back to where the sloop drifted peacefully at her anchor. Saul sat still beside Bill Johnson, his only pal in the gang other than Howlett, who manned the oars. Johnson was far from the smartest bloke in the Fourth Ward, but he'd been nice to Saul from the first day and that went far in Saul's reckoning.

Presently, a small commotion arose towards the back of the ship, a splash and some drunken singing, and the rowboat drifted silently towards the anchor cable. McCarthy was the first to grab hold of it, the cable leading at a slight angle from the black water up to just below the deck. "Bruiser —" he said to Howlett, "— you come next. Want you to take out the guard." Howlett nodded and the gang's captain started climbing.

The others followed like a procession of rats, each one filing behind the last in their preset order. One's hands and head just beneath another's advancing feet and behind. When it was his turn the cable was cold and slick with water between Saul's fingers, but he had strong hands and latched hold easily to lift himself from the rowboat onto the cable. He bent his knees close and squeezed the heels of his boots against the bottom, the East River rushing over his toes some, then pushed with his legs and pulled with his arms higher. He continued until he'd reached the end of the anchor cable and was pulled up the last bit by McCarthy onto the deck. Johnson and one other waited below with the rowboat.

Saul moved with the others down the polished sidedeck within the strange mixture of the night's shadows and the approaching morning. Just ahead, Howlett moved in behind the distracted watchman with his brickbat, a literal slab of brick, carried low. There was a crack, then a groan, then the watchman collapsed as the brickbat crumbled in Howlett's hand. "Might 'ave hit him too hard," McCarthy laughed quietly. "But fine work, Bruiser." He patted the boy on the back and moved with the others into the main cabin. The other crew had now pulled alongside and were being helped up the side with lowered ropes. A dozen Daybreak Boys soon moved about the ship, sifting through its hold and rooms for anything of value.

In the main cabin, Saul and the others had uncovered the small vault hidden behind a rusted weather gauge. Saul worked the lock with his new picks, listened to each tumbler turn while the boys cleared the room of anything of value. "Smith will surely move this along," McCarthy said, holding a small collection of nautical instruments and charts, calculating how much their longtime fencer would pay for the plunder. The gang moved in and out of the room behind him, passing the goods down to the two waiting rowboats.

The lock gave and Saul opened the iron flap. Inside, a bag of bills and a pearl-handled pistol. Payment for the recent delivery. There was plenty for everyone, and McCarthy took the gun and clapped him on the shoulder. Saul thought immediately of Molly and where they might go the next night.

Then the second guard stepped into the room.

But not a guard, Saul decided on second look, one of the sailors. Perhaps the captain of the ship himself, woken by the commotion. Regardless of the title, McCarthy took his new gun and smashed it into the man's head.

124

The man yelped, stumbled to one knee. "Don't," he cried. "Please, you — " McCarthy hit him again.

Still not falling down, he was shoved aside and McCarthy turned to the room. "Move out," he glared. Saul finished emptying the contents of the box into his bag and fell in with the other boys to quickly clear from the room.

Moving though the doorway, he stole a glance at the man who'd found them. There was the white of age in his hair. Blood now ran through his fingers. The hand trembled.

Saul moved out onto the side deck towards the rowboats and a clean escape. A good catch overall, he thought, and tossed the bag down to Johnson in the boat.

A single gun shot rang out behind him.

Several boats in the river sprang to attention. Saul climbed over the railing and turned to see McCarthy step out from the cabin.

A gun battle, Saul thought, tossing the bag of treasure down. *Just like in the stories.*

☠ ☠ ☠

The rest of the crew had already gathered around a rectangular table in the *Hole-in-the-Wall* tavern. The establishment's owner, a one-armed bloke named Charley Mowell, nodded from behind the bar as Saul stepped into the stale, darkened basement and made his way towards them. The others made room when he grabbed a seat and sat down.

"Big ship," McCarthy recapped for Saul. "Up from Florida. Half delivery to New York to be made in two days. The rest to Boston the next."

"What's the prize?"

"Liquor. Sugar. Up from the Caribbean."

"So they'll be half loaded with goods and half with cash."

"And guns," Slobbery Jim added. "Got word they got a whole shipment coming in to take back South."

"Southern pigs."

"A crew of *six* southern pigs, no less."

125

Pints of ale were dropped at the table for the boys. Saul watched the woman move off. Gallus Mag, she was. British giantess over six feet tall. He glanced over at the jar of ears she kept behind the bar. Ears she'd bit off over the years scrapping with unruly customers.

"How to get by a crew that size?" Johnson asked.

"Jimmy's cousin is going to walk us in the front door."

"How's that now?"

"Cause the cotton-lovin' morons hired him as the night's watchman," Slobbery Jim cackled and the table joined him.

"So we tie them up, and make off with it all. Two month's take on one night."

McCarthy shrugged. "A lot of men to hold," he said. "Too much can go wrong. Someone wanting to be a hero like that bloke the other night."

Several around the table laughed. Saul filed away those who had.

"Easiest to just slit 'em while they're sleeping," McCarthy pressed. "And be done with it. Dirty work, men. But better them than me." He lifted his ale in mock toast and the others joined him to drink. Saul had not.

☠ ☠ ☠

"You realize George Washington once lived on this street?" he asked. "*The* George Washington. Right there, in fact."

He stood with her on Cherry Street, the East River running behind them. The usual horde moved through the night around them, spilling from the taverns, gambling houses and dance halls. Molly wore a dress he didn't recognize. He assumed she'd bought it with some of the money he'd been giving her over the weeks.

"I was thinking," he said.

"Yes?" Her eyes wandered the busy street behind him, watching the crowd.

"Met this fellow at the tavern the other night. Might even be a distant cousin, it seems."

"Is that so?"

"Anyhow," he continued. "Seems he fell in with McBride Shipping up on the Hudson. Good pay, he says. Steady work."

She turned to him.

"I thought, maybe, of seeing what that was about."

"You leaving the Daybreak Boys?"

"Me? I don't know. Why would I? Sure. Maybe." He took off his hat, played with the inside. "Good pay, he says. Steady work."

She blew a long whistling sound through her red lips.

"Hey, I know what you're thinking," Saul said. "I ain't daft, see? But, I was thinking that once things settled a bit, I'd still have enough and we could — "

"Look, love," she said and touched a gloved hand to his face. "I needed to talk to you anyway."

He stood frozen in the crowd, caught on her next words.

"I've been seeing someone. Someone else. I've got somewhere else to be tonight."

"Who?"

"James McBeen," she said. "You don't know him."

"The gambler," he smiled darkly. "Sure, I know him. Faro player. I know 'em all down here, *love*."

"Anyways, I don't know what else to say."

"But —"

"It's been real fun and, well, good night now." She patted his hand. "You're a real nice guy." She stepped into the crowd, vanishing into its sea of dark colors and shapes.

For a long time, Saul stood watching the crowd move. It shifted like a river, retreating into the night. He thought of the East River and turned to it. The sun was just rising. Its orange glow seeped over the horizon.

Howlett and Johnson found him still watching it sometime later. A golden ball now lifting over the waterfront, chasing away the dark corners of the night with waves of golden illumination.

"McCarthy told us to fetch ya," Johnson said. "We're going over the plans for tomorrow's hit."

Saul ignored them.

"Hey, what you looking at?" Johnson asked.

"The sunrise," he replied. "Don't think I ever really looked at a sunrise." The two stood behind him, waiting.

"The prettiest damn thing," Saul said, watching it chase away the dark corners of the night. "Just like gold."

"Yeah," Johnson agreed behind him. Howlett beside him.

Saul turned and stepped in with his crew. "And I don't care if I ever see it again," he said.

NOTES: *A police report given to the New York mayor in 1850 estimated some five hundred river pirates split among fifty active gangs. Nicholas Saul and William Howlett became formal captains of the Daybreak Boys in 1850. Under their dual leadership, Saul and Howlett became particularly renowned for their cunning and boldness as the gang pirated more than $100,000 in just two years. The crew also committed some forty murders during this time. Along with their loyal pal Johnson, the two were finally cornered in the Slaughter House Point by twenty heavily-armed policemen who shot it out with the gang and then arrested all three boys for the murder of a dock watchman. Saul and Howlett were hanged in the courtyard of the Tombs in January, 1853. Saul had just turned twenty. More than two hundred attended the hanging, half of whom filed past the scaffold and shook hands with the deceased pirates.*

THE BOAT BENEATH

1864, SOUTH CAROLINA

The other ship was below them.

The first, the doomed *USS Housatonic*, remained above. Ten feet above, remarkably, and a hundred feet away. And through the fogged front porthole and low sloshing waves, Lieutenant George Dixon could still make out its dark shape, perched in the shadowy ocean just ahead. Unwittingly waiting for his attack. Waiting to be sunk by the ultimate weapon. By him.

But the second ship, this *other* ship, this was the one that concerned Dixon now. It was another ten feet below, he figured. An old schooner skewed on its side, mostly buried in dark silt, two masts partially escaping from its shadowed grave like a pair of long gruesome fingers.

Fingers that almost seemed to reach for his submarine. Stretching out to pluck his ship, his men, from the cold black waters and drag them all to the harbor's dim floor.

Dixon smirked. As a child in Indiana, he'd sometimes hold his breath when passing a cemetery for fear that a misplaced soul, a lost ghost, might somehow get inside him. It was a silly superstition his grandmother had taught them. Like black cats and four-leaf clovers. Absurd.

Yet, he now realized he hadn't taken a breath in some time. That he'd trapped the last in his throat waiting until they'd completely passed over the ominous wreckage.

He saw the rusted tips of several cannon aligned across the partially-exposed section of deck and wondered what grand battles the men of the craft might have met. He saw no tattered flag or colors. *Who were they?* Warriors, he assumed. *Men to be recognized. Celebrated.*

His eyes fell back to the masts. Fingers of dark wet bone, he imagined again. And the frayed sails and rigging dangled and fluttered from them like torn grey skin.

Hogwash.

Dixon looked away from the old wreck, shuddering against the sudden and infantile feeling of dread. Deliberately breathing deeply, re-fixed his sights again on the *Housatonic*.

The Union ship remained in position. Its anchor chain had just been slipped, its steam engine now churning water in retreat. *They clearly now suspect.* Rumors of a secret confederate weapon had spread through the harbor all Winter. *Maybe they even see our towers poking out of the waves some.* But too late. She was still dead ahead.

A two hundred footer on the keel, a thousand tons, with a hundred-pounder cannon, ten swivel guns, and a crew of more than a hundred. It was only one ship in the massive Union blockade that strangled Charleston. But it was the largest. And it was a start.

The spar, a spiked seventeen-foot iron pole mounted to the *Hunley's* bow was only feet away now. Its function was simple: rip into the side of the *Housatonic* and deliver the one hundred and thirty pounds of explosives that waited just beneath its tips.

The candle at his right, the only light in the sub, flickered again. The air in the *H.L. Hunley's* cramped hull was rank and hot. Thick. Stifling. It appeared there was barely enough to keep the small flame lit.

He held his pocket watch beside the glow. More than an hour beneath the water, forty minutes left if they remained completely submerged. Four miles out at sea. The walls were dripping from their breath. Dixon thought of telling Becker to put up the snorkel tubes again to let some fresh air back into the sub just in case something went wrong at impact. But they were less than two minutes away.

Instead, he adjusted the diving planes, shifting the tarnished lever and raising the sub some to give the wreck below more clearance. He knew it would expose them more to the *Housatonic* but accepted they'd already been spotted anyway and, more to the point, he didn't want the old masts of a dead ship snagging the spar's rigging.

Because then it all would have been for naught. The weeks of hard training, the cold nights spent blindly moving about the harbor to no avail. Not to mention the other two crews who'd drowned in previous attempts. More than a dozen brave men lost, men Dixon had known and fought beside.

Three knots now, and the team of seven behind him worked the crankshaft at almost full speed. Dixon's back was to them, but he could perfectly visualize their sweat-drenched forms awkwardly hunched over the individual steel cranks. Each man sweltered though surrounded by icy winter waters. Volunteers for the perilous mission, like himself.

The Confederacy, or at the least Dixon and his men, remained hopeful that the strange torpedo boat, the only such ship in the whole world, would ultimately break the blockade of ships that now blockaded the city.

Perilous, indeed. Many had already died trying. Including one of the outlandish vessel's creators. It was improbable at best. But Dixon knew improbable was exactly the kind of bold challenge accepted by any true hero. A trial worthy of Alexander or Achilles.

The steel ship grumbled against the weight of the ocean, long, low groans that filled the iron hull. The deep sound included the rush of the water alongside them and the relentless squawk and rhythm of the crankshaft as it turned the squeaking propeller. The propeller's flywheel and chain clattered. Dixon heard each man's labored breathing. He listened to the water in the front ballast tank splash and burble.

He shivered suddenly, cold despite the stifling conditions in the hull.

Dixon realized they'd fully passed the shipwreck, and he sneaked a final look out the port hole. But, the boat was now lost beneath him, out of sight. He wondered some if he'd actually taken a breath or not.

The mercury gauge near the forward tank read fifteen feet. The compass North East.

The *Housatonic* was within fifty feet. It had moved slightly to the left, but Dixon had tugged *Hunley's* steering rod accordingly. The bar was slippery with his own perspiration.

"Lieutenant?"

The shout had come from Ridgaway, the second-in-command. Sixteen feet away at the back of the sub, six men between them. "Did you — "

"Not now," Dixon shouted back. He pulled the diving-planes lever, rose a few feet. "Full speed!"

He knew Ridgaway had just seen the menacing wreckage too, and wondered quickly what thoughts of terror or alarm might have passed through the Marylander, but there was no time for that.

The *Housatonic* was at thirty feet now, and the Union dogs were shooting at them. The bullets pinged and chimed harmlessly off the *Hunley's* cigar-shaped iron body.

Dixon smiled. *So, they now understand we're not a dolphin or some Fort Sumter jetsam.* He knew they were likely safe from the bullets and that the *Houstanic's* cannons could not target an object so low in the water.

They were at her starboard side, just forward of the mizzenmast. Dixon's hand dropped to his leg to feel the coin in his trouser pocket again.

There was a story among the men that the same coin had once deflected a Yankee bullet at the Battle of Shiloh and saved his life. The Lieutenant was not opposed to the tale, and even helped spread it himself at times. Every great hero had a unique item or legend of some sort he was noted for, some indication of being special. Joan of Arc, Washington, or even Perseus. The coin lent credibility to his ultimate goal.

To be remembered a hero.

The fact that Miss Bennett had given it to him as a keepsake would never mean a thing to anyone. That it had magically stopped a Union bullet meant everything. He was now clearly marked. Born to some grand purpose. He tapped the coin for luck, then crouched deeper in the cramped conning tower and turned quickly to his men.

Their shadowed forms were twisted and lively in the dark hull. They almost looked like storybook dwarves, something beneath the halls of Valhalla shaping Thor's mighty hammer or maybe Odin's spear, *Gungnir*. They hunched over the crankshaft, every ounce of given strength into the final strike. They looked, well, *perfect*, and he was almost afraid to break the moment.

"Rebels!" he cried, "'Tis a patriot's name!" Several heads turned and two men growled spiritedly in reply, but continued cranking. "To Eternity," he said more quietly and then turned back to the viewing window.

Just as the spar rammed into the *Housatonic*.

First, there was a terrible sound. It was the wrenching of wood and steel, the long barbed spear plunging deep into the Union ship. The piercing roar, thought Dixon, of some mythological sea creature.

Then, the *Hunley* lurched forward, every man crashing sideways against the collision. The impact pitched Dixon against his controls and his wrist jammed painfully against the compass. Groans and curses quickly filled the dark hull behind him.

Dixon quickly righted himself in his seat and took hold of the steering rod again. "Reverse," he ordered. His voice was lost in the turmoil of the seats behind. "Reverse, full speed!" he shouted again.

The crank shaft started turning once more. Slowly. The sound of the flywheel and propeller revolving all over again. Turning in reverse. Now pulling the sub *away* from the Union ship.

Dixon yanked a lever attached directly to the spar via a line. It was a movement he'd practiced two dozen times. This time it was for real.

He'd released the explosives.

The sub retreated from the *Housatonic*. Through the port window, he could observe the disorder on the Union vessel. Officers and enlisted alike scrambled every which way. They shouted and pointed. Others continued to shoot harmlessly at the *Hunley's* watch towers as he dropped the dive plane lever and sunk down again.

Bullets popped above them, the sound of something spitting over the sub. All the while, the spar's second line ran out behind them, running off a spool of rope just like one of those new sewing machines. The fact that one of the investors in the *Hunley* was Singer's nephew made Dixon smile all the more.

One hundred and fifty feet until the end of line would play out, and the charge triggered. The sub continued its retreat. Fifty feet away now. Sixty.

"Lieutenant?" It was Ridgaway again.

"Wait, sir."

The view of the *Housatonic* was almost lost to him now, as the tower port completely submerged and the night waters again swallowed the sub. He was chilled again. The air suddenly freezing around him. It felt like the touch of Death itself. And Dixon knew why.

He'd just passed over the boat again.

The boat beneath.

Something about it. Something *foul*.

He'd come across such spots before in this world. As a steamboat engineer sailing the Mississippi River between St. Louis and Cincinnati, there were two he knew of. And just outside Corinth, Mississippi, waiting for the attack at Shiloh, he'd found another in a field beside a forgotten church yard.

These places were icy and lifeless. They'd been tainted somehow with death, and were now devoid of all life. Hidden crypts. Cold pockets of nothing. No, Dixon corrected himself. It was even worse than nothing.

For in these dead spots, the *Nothing* was so deep, so bottomless, it was tangible. It was a nothing you might almost touch if you dared. And it was a nothing that was hungry. Actually hungry. Ravenous even, to pull something alive into it. So that the living thing might join that dreadful nothingness forever.

Eighty feet. One hundred.

Moving backwards over the wreck, the sinister boat soon came back into view in his window. As lifeless and buried as before. Yet, the riggings played in the currents swirling about it.

At one hundred and thirty feet, he watched the last of the line unraveling. "Reverse, full speed," he said again but the words were mumbled, quiet. "Hold on!"

One hundred and fifty. The spar's line had finally run out. There was a brief crackle from somewhere inside the ship. The charge ignited.

"Hold on!"

Then the explosion.

If the sound of the spar ripping into the *Housatonic* was like some mythical sea monster, this noise was like one of mythology's dark angry gods. It was a hideous roar, deafening and vast. Its boom reverberated through the entire sub in a hollow clamor that literally forced Dixon into an anxious crouch.

He waited for the expected aftershock. A rush of water surged towards them in dispersal waves.

The *Hunley* shuddered suddenly, its nose lifting up against the detonation. Freezing water burst free from the forward ballast tank and sprayed over Dixon. The candle extinguished and the sub plunged into chaotic darkness.

The reverberations were more then he'd expected. The *Housatonic* must have been carrying more gunpowder than they'd thought. Stuffed in the ship's hull.

The submarine continued to shake, rocking wildly into an angle Dixon didn't recognize. He crashed backward, slamming into one of the other men. They both fell and all sense of direction was slammed, lost, in the cold darkness.

Water surged over him, Dixon's hands grasping for either the sub's wall or floor. Alarmed voices shouted out in the black. His hands slipped against the slick wall, but he fought back to his feet, somehow grabbing hold of the steering rod. Couldn't understand why it felt so odd.

Dixon now realized they were about to completely flip over.

In the dark, he lunged for the hand pump to release the water in the forward ballast tank. If he could just empty the tank in time, the sub might correct itself. The upended boat wobbled cruelly and his hands fumbled blindly over the controls until he'd found it.

The sub tersely grunted in a low metallic rumble as its back drove into the sandy ocean floor. Water sprang from the gloom. It squirted from unseen seams and cracks across his back and face. The hiss of the pump ejecting water from the tank joined the spluttering leaks.

"Forward!" he shouted over the din. "Half speed!"

Dixon didn't know if anyone had even heard him or what they might do if they had. The sub's new and unfamiliar clanks and squeaks now surrounded him. He would have sworn the boat was literally splitting apart. Would the propeller even turn? Had it been damaged in the aftershock?

His other hand pulled down on the dive plane control. The cold copper quavered back against his fingers and fought his control. He'd lost the peculiar sense of being shoved backward and then felt the ship settle more horizontally. With the sound of the explosion past, he now distinctly heard the propeller grinding again, the crankshaft turning.

"Half speed!" he ordered again. "Let's bring her up."

The sub shifted forward again, leveled itself. Dixon had worked himself back into the captain's chair and, even in the dark, recovered full control of the ship. Dixon couldn't see the depth gauge, but knew they were rising. He yanked the steering rod, and the boat began a slow turn forward.

Outside the porthole, the harbor was cloudy and mottled in shadow. Sand and silt blasted from the ocean floor now swirled within the dark waves.

And something else.

A shape large and angular. A great grey thing hovering in the swirling cloud of darkness and silt. Its sharp lines were etched within shafts of approaching moonlight.

A sail.

Dixon squinted into the darkness, kept turning the sub.

It was the sunken ship. The wreck. The explosion had somehow jostled it loose. Its bow was now freed from the sand and pointed directly at his own ship. The shimmer of tattered masts flapped directly behind it as if it were moving.

The dark water swayed and confused as shadow and settling silt drifted through the water.

He saw movement on its forward deck.

Not possible.

Shapes moving across it. Shapes oddly human.

He saw a pennant now. A long black flag suspended along the mast in the stirred under currents. Within the iridescent moon beams, it showed a jawbone-less skull over a wide curved sword.

Dixon looked away, breathed harshly in the greasy air. He pulled harder on the steering rod, though the sub could turn no faster. He grabbed the dive planes a final time.

Pirates?

The light grew brighter in his port window. Dixon could see the surface. The sub's nose lifted from the water with a belched moan. At last, the ship settled again at the top of the ocean.

An actual sunken pirate ship.

He turned to the others. The submarine was half filled with light again. It was moonlight only, and the moon's pastel glow was dim and shrouded in gloomy February clouds, but it was good enough. They'd been too long in the dark.

Dixon smiled. The men had stopped turning the crank even though he'd not told them to. He supposed they'd earned it. They, too, had probably never expected to reach the top again. "Becker, put the snorkel tubes up." He tapped the man on the shoulder. "Get some fresh air. It's still a bit of a trip home."

Becker grinned in the moonlight. "Aye, aye, sir." He looked tired, drained.

"Is everyone well?" Dixon asked. The men all grunted in agreement. "Ridgaway?" He called to the back of the sub over the other huddled shapes.

"Hurt my shoulder a bit, sir," his second shouted back. "Be crankin' with one hand home, sir."

"Thank you, Mr. Ridgaway," Dixon said. "That's just fine."

Waves quietly lapped over the top of the sub and splashed against its two towers. The boat rocked gently in the waves.

"Did it work?" one of the men asked softly.

For the first time in a long while, Dixon thought of their mission. He peered slowly out the side port window. He breathed a heavy sigh and the sound filled the curious and quiet hull.

The *Housatonic* was engulfed in flames and sinking fast. Dozens of escape dinghies floundered in water around it. Dixon checked his pocket watch again. It had been no more than three minutes since the explosion.

He chuckled softly now. They'd done it.

They'd actually sunk the *Housatonic.*

He was shocked at how surprised that realization left him. He'd always spoken as if their success were assured. But now, they'd really done it. And the mission would soon transform the entire war. With another sub, maybe two, Dixon imagined the Charleston blockade could be broken in a matter of weeks. Surely, once General Beauregard heard the news, the funds would be found for more "fish boats."

Dixon smiled at the nickname. It had been given as a joke, but all that was about to change. The "joke" had worked. The *Hunley,* its crew and its captain, would forever be the first submarine in the history of warfare to sink an enemy ship! That was assuredly only the start. Who knew what further success awaited him? From the 21st Alabama infantry to assignments with the Confederate Special Services, and now this. His career was assured now, certainly. They were genuine Heroes.

"Yes," he reported, hoping his voice didn't crack. "It worked. She'll be at the bottom in another minute."

The men broke out in cheer behind him. Their voices were tired and cracked, but it was a cheer nonetheless, and he even recognized a genuine southern battle yelp amid the sudden ovation. The infamous call, feared throughout the North, was almost otherworldly echoing about the tiny submarine.

Dixon lit the blue magnesium light and held it against the window towards the shore four miles away. The ground crew back at Breach Inlet on Sullivan's Island would see the signal and know they were alive and well. They'd prepare for the *Hunley's* triumphant return. "Half speed," he ordered. "Let's get her home."

The men cheered briefly once more and stared churning the crank again. Dixon suddenly wished he could join them but knew his role at the front well enough. The propeller clanged back into action and the ship crept slowly forward.

The distinct sound of cannon fire boomed suddenly across the sub. Dixon turn round to view the *Housatonic.*

The Union ship had all but vanished and was quite a distance away again. Too far to reach them. A large cloud of black smoke and sputtering flame lifted from its small dark outline. Its cannons were several feet underwater by now.

He turned to all port windows and looked for another ship, a second Union vessel that had fired at them. The ocean appeared tranquil and empty.

Again the cannon sound echoed through the sub. This time, it resounded with a heavy thud that literally shook the *Hunley*.

"We're hit," one of the men shouted.

Water sprang from the bottom corner of the forward tanks, splurted into the hull. Dixon spun around again, looking for the attacking ship. He could not see it. "Prepare to dive!" he shouted out. The others groaned at his decision. "Mr. Becker, keep the blasted snorkels up. We're not going down too far. Just enough." Just down enough to evade whatever ship was firing at them.

"Aye, Aye, sir."

Water sloshed over the ship's floor. "Forget the crank," he told Becker. "And try and pump some of this out," he added.

At Dixon's handling, the *Hunley's* towers vanished again beneath the dark waters. "Blast," he cursed and listened to the water rush over the top of the sub.

He now heard shouting.

Voices in the water. The sound was low and distant but it was definitely human.

"What is that, Captain," Becker whispered.

Dixon shook his head.

He thought of the *Housatonic* and wondered how many men had perished in the attack. Were there still survivors trapped in the ship? Was he really hearing their anguished voices from so far away?

"Avast," one of the men, Carlsen, said suddenly.

Dixon crouched to see him. "What?"

"I — It sounded like someone was saying —"

"Who?" Becker demanded, pumping out the water. More seemed to fill the boat despite his efforts. "Who said it?"

"*Avast.*"

Dixon heard it now too.

The sound was wet. It *dripped.*

He thought suddenly of a jawbone-less skull over a wide curved sword.

Dixon peered from the window and saw the other ship at last.

The ship had two masts, with a large square mainsail and a diamond-shaped topsail on the mainmast, and a small foresail, with an empty bowsprit. The masts were misty and wraithlike. Her gun deck was forty feet on the keel with a beam of thirteen feet. Dixon counted twelve guns. The ship glimmered in the water, shimmering between streaks of moonlight and shadow. "Captain, what is it?"

Bodies moved along the unnatural ship. The wispy specters flickered between real men and something else. Bone poked through rotted clothing.

"Dixon!"

Dixon watched as one of the cannons fired. Something snaked through the water over the sub. "Full speed!" he shouted. "Full speed ahead!"

The men turned the crank as one and something in Dixon's voice had them moving the sub faster than it had ever gone before.

It wouldn't be fast enough.

The terrible ship followed on their heels and shapes now emerged from its rotted hull, and they moved as one towards the sub. Their vaporous bodies moved easily through the water and their shouts came from faces half-covered beneath hats and beards in the shadow. The faces were skeletal.

"Men, prepare —" Dixon didn't know for what exactly. "— Prepare for battle."

The others looked confused as Dixon pulled his pistol from its holster.

Hands now reached up from under the sub. They simply lifted through the iron hull.

The hands were spectral, wisps of lustrous smoke that lifted into the hull and hardened into sea-green bone. The fingers were misshapen and sodden. Dark splintered nails grew sharply from the tips. They grabbed several of the men. Screaming filled the hull.

A full figure suddenly pushed through the side of the sub. It wore a short decayed jacket and a rotting scarf around its exposed spine. It had a long dark beard, twisted into black ribbons and two pairs of pistols hung from its crooked shoulders.

"*Avast,*" the eerie figure demanded again. Sea water trickled from its throat over blackened gums and down its chin.

Dixon lifted his pistol and fired at the horrific figure. The bullet burst through its chest with a damp splurt. It smiled, a skull's grin rotted and ghastly, as it vanished back into the ocean.

The port window had shattered, water rushing through the crack. Dixon pulled the dive planes to lift the sub again, then squinted into the chaos in the rest of the sub.

Frank Collins, the biggest man on the crew, wrestled hand to hand with one of the unearthly forms. The thing had only half emerged from the bottom of the sub so that Dixon could only see it from the waist up. It carried a curved dagger in its boney jaw.

Collins kicked the creature in its face and teeth scattered off the far wall. Water now spurted beneath Collin's shadowed form.

Something grabbed at Dixon's face and he shoved it away. It had been something cold, crooked, and dripping.

Dixon watched as more shapes slithered from the dark water over the top of the submarine. The boat felt too heavy. It wasn't climbing. In fact, he found that, during the struggle, the water had now risen to his waist.

Forms and shadows splashed through the overcrowded hull. He watched Ridgaway fall across the crank and onto another demonic form that'd sunk claws into Lumpkin. The Marylander stuck at the creature with his fists, but was tossed back with a vicious swipe of the apparition's club. He fell back, holding his shattered nose. Collins now leapt into the fray.

Becker struggled with several hands that had come through the top of the sub and yanked to pull him into the Atlantic. Dixon lunged into the water at the skeletal arms and tugged at them to release. Several bone fingers snapped off in his hand, and he collapsed back into his own area.

He found it harder to move now. The water tickled up his neck, rising over his chin. It ran across his trembling lips. Salty and cold.

It occurred to him now that there would likely be no parades or advancement. Large crowds would never actually cheer his name. He would soon be forgotten, another name lost in an ever-growing list.

More ethereal hands reached into the sub, grabbing.

He was standing now, his face pressed against the roof of his navigation tower. He breathed only through his nose now as the icy water rolled up past his mouth.

Through the cracked port window, a face now appeared from out of the dark water. It moved towards him through the ocean. Black eye sockets beneath the wide feathered hat. The water gurgled over Dixon's ears.

He thought of Miss Bennett and clutched her coin to his chest. For years, he'd imagined her gift as a talisman, a sign of greater things to come. Now he realized it had only been a mark of what he already had. And he found that thought quite pleasing. He hoped she would remember him.

An emerald blade glimmered in the ocean.

Then, he thought of his grandmother. His grandmother and her amusing superstitions. Dixon liked to think she might be somehow pleased. Flattered.

Because as the ghostly thing seized him, he was already holding his breath.

NOTES: *Not until World War I, fifty years later, would another submarine sink an enemy ship. The pioneering H.L. Hunley never returned from its fateful mission that night and the mystery of its disappearance baffled historians for more than one hundred years. Finally, in 1995, after a fourteen-year search, novelist and adventurer Clive Cussler and divers from his nonprofit National Underwater and Marine*

Agency found her at the bottom of Charleston Harbor, 1000 feet away from where she'd sunk the USS Housatonic.

All eight men were found at their positions within the submarine. Lieutenant George Dixon's gold coin was discovered amid his possessions (as was an engagement ring) and forensics of the dented coin have since proven that the story of the blocked bullet was true. On April 17, 2004, the remains of the entire crew were finally laid to rest in Charleston's Magnolia Cemetery with full military honors, in a service attended by as many as 10,000. To this day, no one knows why the H.L. Hunley *sank.*

AND A BOTTLE OF RUM

1928, NEW JERSEY

The boat's captain was obviously insane. It showed in his scarlet stockings and frilly silk shirt, and in the braided ringlets of dark hair beneath his strange high hat. It showed in the ridiculous way he talked and in the insufferable parrot clinging to his left shoulder, cackling about "pieces of eight" and the like. But mostly, Recinella decided, it showed in the man's guns.

This dope, one Captain Barbary, carried two flintlock pistols, each wedged into a wide leather belt, a couple of bean-shooters men might have used even before the Civil War. The kind of piece you had to load with powder and a bullet each and every time you wanted to shoot. It was moronic! In contrast, Recinella's beloved Thompson was known to put out more than a thousand shots in a quick minute. Even the .38 strapped beneath his jacket held six and had a double-action trigger. This line of work simply tolerated nothing less.

So, Recinella was a bit disappointed with the guy's hardware. He'd expected more. Word was this mook was one of the best rum runners in the game, a real prince of the East coast. Apparently ran five separate ships along Rum Row, had a dozen Coast Guard captains in his back pocket, and could move six thousand cases of booze a week. Pulling in closer to three hundred grand a year while the "Average Joe" made six. There were even rumors he'd been part of the crew who'd iced old Salvatore Falcone, one of Chicago's major gangsters.

So, he was a real player. Someone worth recruiting. Only two problems with the guy. Problem One, he ran for some of the boys in Chicago. The Philly organization, with whom Recinella had regular employment, had other plans for the runner. And Problem Two, he was *stugatze*, the worst kind of insane. While the rest of the small crew dressed like typical longshoremen, this one thought he was some kind of Hollywood pirate. Hoop earring, tattoos, cuffed black leather boots.

To address Problem One, Recinella was now stuck fifteen miles somewhere off the coast of North Jersey in the middle of the night on the *Tipostrano*, a sodden, seventy-foot wreck of a sailboat that had no business being on the water. Yet, thanks to Prohibition, that same wreck now carried a $200,000 delivery of whiskey below decks, a delivery straight from Canada to some secret inlet in South Jersey.

Joey Knuckles was with him, there for the talking part. And Recinella, well, Recinella was there for "expediting the negotiations" if the talking thing didn't work out as hoped.

It hadn't come to that yet, and for that Recinella was unusually thankful. He could barely stand, yet alone "negotiate." Just trying to stay on his feet, trying harder still not to puke again. The short Stutter-tub ride out to the ship had been bad enough, but the sea itself was almost unbearable. It seemed as if the whole world had swung off its hinges.

There was constant movement as the boat swayed and dropped beneath him on endless undulating waves. He eyed the swells from the deck, his hands clenched tightly around the railing, biting mist in his face. He was trapped in its never-ending vertigo, and it grew utterly nauseating. Recinella kept focused on the ridiculous pistols, ignoring the ongoing urge to vomit as everything dipped and rocked around him, and the other two men somehow continued to talk.

"It's costing 'em an extra fifteen, maybe twenty percent in transport alone," Joey explained as the Captain stood beside him, obviously only half-listening as he watched his men scurry about the ship. "Driving the goods halfway 'cross the friggin' country. Makes no sense, see. Oughta be crossing at Canada or over the Lakes."

146

"Sailin's no good on the Lakes, mate."

"All I'm saying," Joey pressed, "is that it's wasted profit that, if you was working for us, could be going directly into your —"

"Come now, Mr. Recinella!" the burly figure turned suddenly and bellowed into the wind. "It's nigh time we showed ye 'bout hoistin' the jib sail."

Recinella cringed. The clown had been on his case since they'd first stepped aboard the boat, pointing out various sails and lines and hunks of timber Recinella didn't give two rats' behinds about. He'd even tossed a rope at Recinella at one point, and taught him to tie something called a "half hitch" and a "sheep" something. Good enough knots to learn, Recinella supposed, but nothing more than a distraction from the business at hand.

"Ye fix a brilliant knot, Mr. Recinella," the captain had told him.

The gangster had shrugged, his smile cold. "Sometimes a man needs a good knot. Certain situations, if you know what I mean."

"I do, mate," the rum runner had grinned back. "I do indeed."

And now to the sail. Recinella's hands felt brittle and clumsy on the rope as he helped yank it high into the darkness above. The wind abruptly caught hold of the sail and it unfurled entirely with the black flag of skull and crossbones flapping just above.

"*Hoistin' the jib,*" the parrot echoed suddenly, cackling. "*Hoistin' the jib.*"

Joey Knuckles smirked beside them as the ship dipped again and Recinella grabbed the line to steady himself.

"Ships ahoy!" someone shouted from the front of the ship. "Two fer."

"As e'er," the captain gruffed. "Better be securin' that line," he added and goaded Recinella into a final tug before one of the other men tied the rope down. "Can't be too quiet with lines flappin in the wind."

"What's the problem?"

"Feds be waitin' just past thar' point, see," he pointed to the mark inland and led the two men up to the quarter deck and the immense wood steering wheel. "Two patrol boats 'bout three miles off the shore."

"Can we outrun them?" Joey Knuckles stared off into the vast darkness before them. Recinella couldn't see anything yet either.

"Won't have to," the captain replied, staring over the wheel at the same dark sea. "Rained last night, February rain. See it hangin' off the coast?"

Recinella followed his gaze. "The fog?"

The captain smiled. "Aye, matey."

"*Ghosts in the mist*," the bird squealed. "*Ghosts in the mist.*" The sound was unbearable and Recinella fought the urge to reach for his gun.

Joey Knuckles steadied his partner's notorious instincts with a warning glare, then winked. "What's the plan, Captain," he asked.

"Take her in frightful close, see," he said. "Got maybe four feet to play with 'long that line. Shoal's deeper than they think. Fasten those lines!" he hissed suddenly over the deck, and the crew of six scrambled back into action. "Flappin' sails and riggin no good for this," he scrutinized the mast above them. "Keep her taut."

"Sneak right past 'em, huh." Joey Knuckles understood first. "We quiet enough for that, Captain?"

"Over their bloody engines?" The captain smiled and adjusted the wheel some into the wind as the ship sped forward into the approaching mist. The flicker of lights now appeared in the distance and Recinella imagined the dark shape of a federal patrol boat between them. The *Tipostrano* kept its course straight towards the coastline. "There be some foul shoals and berms in there," the Captain pointed.

"Isn't that dangerous?" Recinella asked. The first vapors of grey mist had already crept over the front of the ship.

"Of course it is, matey," the Captain checked the compass by the wheel. "And that's why the feddies be keepin' away." The mist stretched over the ship, absorbed it, until the bow, just thirty feet ahead, had almost vanished completely. The mast had already disappeared in a ghastly combination of darkness and fog, and the lights from the patrol boats, Recinella noticed, were also gone now.

Even so, the mist continued to rush over the deck and then quickly enfolded the rest of the ship. The fog proved somehow warm and silky against Recinella's raw wind-worn face. The crew had grown quiet around him, motionless across the deck, and endless sheets of the stuff now hovered at every turn. He recognized the distinct sound of water sloshing along the ship's hull. He could hear the wind in the sails. "Waste of time," he huffed, and one of the crew hushed him.

"How do you see where you're going?" Joey Knuckles asked quietly. His voice sounded distant in the ghost-like mist.

The captain chuckled, "Bit of sailor's luck, matey. And perhaps," he eyed the compass secured beside the wheel. "A wee bit of sense. Can't ye hear the breakers?"

Joey Knuckles shrugged.

"The waves," the captain explained proudly. "We'll just keep her on this tack until I don't hear 'em no more, then break out southeast a mile past the coppers." Recinella watched the mist dance over the captain's hat and shoulders. At the crook of his neck, the detestable bird huddled tightly in the haze. "Reading?" the man called out suddenly.

"Fifteen, Captain," came the hushed reply, and the captain nodded as if it was what he'd expected to hear. To Recinella, it simply looked as if the men had pulled a bucket from the side of the ship. Then they dropped it in again.

Something fluttered above them in the mist, and the captain pointed silently, fiercely, forward. Several men adjusted their lines until he waved them away again. All the while, his eyes darted about the craft, studying the compass and sails, leering over the bow into the eerie mist.

The *Tipostrano* moved in virtual silence through the mist. The minutes passed. Except for water running beside the boat, only the captain made a sound. It was low humming, the bare hint of a melodic tune escaping from underneath his shaggy beard. "What's that," Recinella asked, cold and irritated.

"Just an old sea shanty, Mr. Recinella," the captain smiled. "Something to pass the time." Then he sang out loud, grinning in the dark. "*Whiskey is the life of man, always was since the world began. Whiskey-o, Johnny-o, Rise her up from down below, Whiskey, whiskey, whiskey-o.*"

Sounds like some Paddy lullaby, thought Recinella, quite sorry he'd brought it up at all. The captain stopped singing after another verse and adjusted the wheel some. "Mr. Dartnel," he said calmly, "Please take the helm and keep her on this tack until I return. The jib halliard's slacked off some."

"Aye, aye, Captain." Another man appeared from the mist and took the wheel and the rum runner waved the two to follow. "Let us retire to quarters for further discussion, mates," he said.

Joey Knuckles and Recinella followed slowly behind, Recinella's legs particularly unsteady atop the rolling ship. He was relieved to get his hands upon the railing leading down steps to the Captain's quarters and even more so when they crowded into a drab, shadowy room and discovered a chair to collapse into. He shook out his hat and brushed the wet from his shoulders, hoping to chase away the coldness in his bones while the captain adjusted his lanterns and the small room filled with carroty light.

"So, you live on this boat, captain?" Joey Knuckles asked, looking about. The walls were showered in maps and teeming shelves of junk. There was a short table equally crowded in paperwork and nautical paraphernalia neither man recognized.

"Most time," the captain held out his elbow so the lime-colored bird could walk down the length of his arm to a brass perch, where it also shook out the sea from its feathers. The rum runner then sat across from the two men with a heavy sigh.

"Where's home then?"

"Nowhere, really. The sea, I suppose. We get about, don't ye know."

"Where you from originally?" Recinella asked.

"Bristol, England" the captain replied, smiling. "But under sail quite early. Let's talk then, mates."

Joey offered his finest smile. "You're the best," he started. "And, quite frankly, we think you can do better for yourself working with us. I know we'd do better." The captain only scratched at his thick graying beard in reply, so Joey pushed on. "That's why Mr. Capuzzi sent us out to speak with you."

"You want me rum, eh?"

"That's the part the feds just don't get." Joey laughed. "*Everyone* wants your rum, Captain. No law's ever gonna change that fact."

The parrot squawked suddenly. "*Yo ho ho, Fifteen men. Yo ho ho.*"

"What's that?" Recinella asked. His voice sounded strained and clipped, even to his own ears. He eyed the bird with open hatred now.

"Another old song, Mr. Recinella," the captain explained, singing lightly. "*Fifteen men on a dead man's chest, Yo ho ho and a bottle of rum.*"

"What's it supposed mean?"

The captain only grinned back and the parrot cackled again.

"We're offering fifteen percent —," Joey pushed ahead, "— above what you're making now."

The rum runner ran dirty fingers along the arm of his chair. "You'd mentioned twenty."

Joey winked at Recinella, who nodded back awkwardly, grimly. Despite the fact he was finally sitting down, the hitman's entire body remained in torturous motion. The boat continued its drops and erratic bobbles even though he couldn't see them from inside the cabin. He just felt them now. And that, Recinella thought with clammy dismay, actually somehow made things even worse. His need to upchuck had doubled.

His eyes darted nervously about the cramped cabin, looking for distraction, for something, *anything*, to focus and just maybe take his mind of his churning stomach and the boat's own loathsome movements. As Joey and the wannabe-pirate talked indirectly about money and potential quantities, Recinella continued his cyclic search of the cabin. He rediscovered framed maps and knickknacks, dark capes hung from a rack, a monstrous wooden mask from some foreign shore displayed against one wall, wide-feathered hats, and ornate swords best left for the picture shows. There was a short table covered in maps, several small leather pouches and —

And just underneath the desk, in a small shadowed compartment, was a small chest. A treasure chest, Recinella thought mockingly. Why not? *An actual treasure chest.*

While Joey continued to sing the captain's praises, working him towards another offer, Recinella continued to work over the matter of the chest, successfully keeping his mind of the ship's tossing and the dull conversation.

The chest looked old, aged red wood with dark hinges and covered in brass decorations of sailing ships, the moon and stars. It measured maybe two feet long and two feet high. Its latch, like the infantile ornamentation, was outlined in gold.

But as for inside the chest, Recinella could now only guess. Cash, likely. Or guns. Maybe just photos of some dame or the captain's prized collection of Paul Whiteman records. Stacks of actual gold coins seemed most likely.

"I'm satisfied where I be, mates."

It sounded like the conversation had taken a turn and Recinella looked away from the chest.

Joey dropped his head to play with his hat. "No disrespect, Captain, but the Falcone family just ain't what it used to be. And you know it. Heck, everyone knows it. Since Big Sal, well — His son's a good-enough kid but —"

"Frankie is doing just fine," the Captain corrected him and Joey held out his hands apologetically.

Recinella'd had it with Joey's approach. "Heard you mighta whacked his old man," he cut in.

Joey laughed nervously and turned to him, but Recinella continued.

"Heard old Sal came out here to take a look around and fell into some foul characters. Still ain't found his body."

The captain only chuckled in reply. "They say you should believe none of what you hear and only half of what you see."

Recinella smiled back. "And, what'd you see?"

"We're not really interested in the past, Captain," Joey stepped in carefully between the two. "Only the future, and the Falcone family might not have one."

The captain's eyes gleamed in interest. "Is that so?"

Joey leaned forward. "I'm not at liberty to discuss the specifics, of course. But I can tell you that change is a natural, and necessary, element of all good business. We'd like you to be part of that change."

Recinella glanced at the chest again. That's it, he thought smugly. Maybe it holds the very bones of one Salvatore Falcone, infamous boss of Chicago.

"Your boys making a move into Chicago, are ye? What about Bugs Moran and Hymie Weiss? Chicago has – "

"I can say only that we're interested in more than the greater Philadelphia area and have worked out certain matters with specific Chicago interests. But —," he held up a finger "— Let's not concern ourselves with Chicago. Your merchandise has a better future along the East Coast. I think —"

"Pardon me, Captain." One of the other sailors had appeared in the doorway.

"What is it?"

"Two new ships spotted northeast."

"Feds?"

"Unknown, Captain. They haven't moved towards us yet."

The captain rose from his chair with a grunt and placed the towering black hat on his head again. "If you gentlemen will excuse me," he said. "I'd best be takin' a look."

"Should we come up?" Joey asked.

"Stay warm and dry," the captain patted a reassuring hand on his shoulder. "I'll hail ye if it turns out to be anything special." He then followed the other sailor out the door and shut it behind him.

"What do you think?"

Recinella shook his head, watched the doorway. "We don't need this clown."

"He's good."

"He's a nut job. Thinks he's Douglas-flippin'-Fairbanks. If you gonna go Hollywood, Joey, better we find a wannabe Greta Garbo." Recinella looked around. "Who ever heard of rum running on a stinkin' sailboat?"

"He got past those coppers well enough."

"I say we off him right now."

"Now *you're* nuts."

"You told him all 'bout Chicago. If he don't take the deal tonight, you got no choice. He'll go to lil' Falcone and ruin everything."

"Maybe. Look, if he don't warm up soon, I'll have you work with him in your own persuasive style. Let him know what's what. Think you can handle that?"

"You keep me round for my smile?"

"You really think he killed Falcone?"

Recinella shrugged, but his eyes passed over the treasure chest. "Let's find out." It was almost close enough to grab.

"What's that?"

Recinella stood up, moved towards the chest.

"What are you doing"

"Quiet, ya mook. Just watch the door." He crouched to get a better look at the latch and its small lock. "I wanna see what pirate boy's hiding."

"Get outta there, you dumb ape." Joey fidgeted behind him. "You gonna ruin everything."

"One second." Recinella pulled out his knife and flipped out the blade to work the lock. "Just need —"

From the corner of his eye, then, he noticed the parrot again. The bird remained in the corner of the room on its perch, head cocked, coolly staring back at the two men with one huge eye. The eye was almost human in its interest. Watching.

Recinella found he'd stopped. "You think that stupid thing really talks?" he asked.

"Beats me," Joey sat back down slowly. "Just get in your chair."

"Well, then what's it staring at me for?" He stepped away from the desk towards the bird with his blade. "Bet ya parrot taste just like chicken, yeah?"

"Yo ho ho," the bird screeched again suddenly, and the hitman jumped backwards with a curse. "Dead man's chest. Yo ho ho." Its wings flapped furiously.

"Nice work, Tarzan," Joey Knuckles laughed. "You're a natural."

"Who's Tarzan?" Recinella glared at the now-preening parrot. "I'm gonna skin that bird alive."

"You'll get your chance soon enough," Joey said and refit his hat on his head. "To tell ya the truth, I'm gettin' a little tired of the pirate act myself. How 'bout you take over the discussions when our man gets back. As a demonstration, you can start with the bird if you like."

"It's about damn time."

Footsteps grew just outside the doorway, and Recinella moved slowly back in his chair as the door opened with a whoosh of cold air as the captain stepped in. "Best be headin' up now, mates. Things be gettin' interesting."

"What's the problem?" Joey jumped up and followed the direction of the captain's arm to the stairs.

"'Tis the feds afterall, don't ye know."

"Not your guys?"

"Me mates?" he held out his other arm for the parrot and the bird crossed the room in a single swoop of its wings. "No, not mine." He scratched the parrot's head gently. "These boats look to be down from New York. Don't answer our signals."

Recinella moved to join them, but not without another quick glance at the chest. *Something very important in there, ain't that right Captain?*

He stepped clumsily back into the blustering weather and followed the men up to the quarter deck. The lights of several ships, more federal patrol boats no doubt, closed in the distance.

"How long before they get here?" Joey asked over the din of wind and rigging.

The captain checked the sails. "Maybe five minutes."

"We should dump the booze."

"What for, matey? You Philadelphia boys were always so quick to dump and run. Afraid of gettin' pinched, is it?"

Joey muttered an oath. "More mist, then, Captain?"

"Come now, Mr. Recinella!" he waved suddenly. "It's nigh time we showed ye 'bout helmin' the wheel."

Recinella sighed. "I don't think —"

"*Capt'n at the wheel*," the parrot cawed harshly, "*Capt'n at the wheel!*"

"Come now," the captain made room for Recinella to step forward as the other sailor moved away from the massive wood wheel. "Helming a ship is somethin' every man should do once in his life. And this hand's needed elsewhere."

Recinella moved forward slowly, and resolved that when he was done with the bird, he'd move quickly to the captain himself. He took hold of the wheel. "What now?"

The captain moved in behind him and Recinella felt the man's weight against his back and arms. "Hold her steady," the gruff voice told him. "She's marked on the compass, see."

Recinella found the compass ahead of the wheel, watched the needle bobbing within.

"Keep her on this tack," he felt the captain tugging at his arms. "Losing wind, mate! Don't over steer her now."

Recinella ignored the captain's prodding and hovering presence as best he could and focused on keeping the boat steady. *If this fool could do it, how hard could it be?* He glared at the compass, watching the needle. It had already become annoying, boring. Nerve wracking. "You actually enjoy this?" Recinella said.

"More than anything," The rum runner replied quietly behind him. "Once, only a boy's dream. Fortunately, I finally discovered the sea's always been in my blood, matey. That I belong here."

Recinella turned to see the captain's face, and the man just smiled back at him. "I think I'm done here now, Mr. Recinella. Keep her on this tack, I'll be back quicker than ye can say Jack Robinson."

"Where you going?"

"Time to roll out the guns," he grinned. "On the line!" He shouted out and bodies jumped across the ship. "On the line!" In reply, the bird at his shoulder clucked excitedly.

As Recinella watched, the crew pulled away several canvas tarps to uncover a dozen small cannons on either side of the boat. Each one nestled within a frame of dark wood, where the cast iron muzzles already glistened in the sea's night air. The federal revenue ships, no doubt carrying modern machine guns, closed in.

Recinella found his hand tight on the wheel, inelegantly wiping the mist from his face with the other. Facing arrest was bad enough, but he'd learned to live with that over the years. It was the idea of the compass terrified him now, he realized. If he were off by only a few degrees, would they hit the shore? Crash and sink? With both hands back on the slick wheel, the dark ocean gave way before him, and the nose of the *Tipostrano* continued its charge into the endless darkness.

"Give me a hand, matey," he heard the captain order behind them and Joey Knuckles moved to help. Recinella snuck a nervous peek and found the two men working at a large tarp at the back of the ship. Another cannon perhaps.

It was an engine.

"Is that —"

"Keep her steady now, Mr. Recinella!" the captain shouted, freeing the rest of the tarp, and Recinella turned grudgingly back to the wheel.

Behind him, the boat's engine snarled into action and the deafening sound directly swallowed any noise of wind in the sails and clattering rigging. Recinella was glad to hear it. He felt the entire ship hesitate only a moment, the propeller establishing a determined footing in the ocean, then thrust forward. It had already almost doubled its speed. Now the darkness wedged away on either side in only fleeting glimpses of waves and mist. Recinella gawked wide-eyed at the compass.

"Prime the cannons!" The captain shouted, jumping forward on the deck. "Mr. Shields, take the helm. Hard east."

"Aye, aye, sir." One of the crew had already appeared at Recinella's side to grab hold of the wheel. Recinella stepped away, found that his hands were shaking. The ship swung sharply to the left, pitching sideways, heeling over towards the shore. Recinella stumbled, grabbing hold of the railing, the sea spewing water across his legs and face. Sails reset and snapped back into place atop the three masts. The federal boats had moved within just half a mile.

"Prepare to fire!" The captain moved back to the engine and grabbed hold of a badly-stained bucket. He then slowly poured its dark content over the engine's exposed exhaust manifolds.

"Smoke screen." Recinella stumbled carefully towards the back of the ship. "Make your own mist."

"Aye," the captain said, applying more of the oil. "A slight diversion for our friends."

Almost immediately, a cloud of black smoke had formed at the back of the ship. The oily smog was thick and dark, and it quickly spread out behind them like a billowing storm cloud. The Coast Guard patrol boats were shortly lost behind it.

"Fire at will!" the captain yelled.

The ship jerked suddenly, backed with a thunderous boom that surpassed even the engine. Recinella ducked defensively and another blast quickly sounded somewhere within the darkness. The air filled with acrid smoke. The crew worked quickly, moving to other cannons. From the tips of several muzzles, flashes of fire spit into the night. Each time, another booming explosion.

Behind them, Recinella made out the distinct sound of return fire. Scores of bullets whizzed and splashed in the water to their far right.

The captain looked out over the bow of the ship. "In all this smoke, the sound's usually enough to chase 'em off. If not..." he pulled back the tarp.

Beneath waited a mounted machine gun. Top of the line, navy issue that Recinella recognized immediately. A fifty caliber Browning, offering a thousand rounds per minute. This wasn't any powder-primed kid's gun.

"Holy Moses!"

"Aye, matey," the captain grinned, stepping behind the gun. "U.S. jurisdiction ends twelve miles that way," he pointed ahead towards the deep sea, the darkness. "We'll surely reach the Rum Line before they can regroup. Drop the sails!"

He triggered the machine gun and its deafening roar joined the other boisterous sounds of battle. Aiming blindly into the dark cloud of smoke, hundreds of bullets spat like frantic screams from the trembling muzzle. Spent shells popped and clacked off the deck at their feet. It was the first sound Recinella had really recognized in hours.

The cannon fire ended as the crew worked the sails, lowering them quickly and tying them off. Once tied, they moved quickly back to the steaming guns. The short explosions resumed.

"Full speed ahead!" the captain roared, and the parrot stomped and paced nervously at his shoulder.

The engine revved, wailing shrilly, and the *Tipostrano* lurched forward again. It shot ahead deeper into the ocean, slicing through the lurching waves, four times the speed as before. Recenilla grabbed hold of the slick railing again. The black smoke cloud quickly fell away behind them.

"What you got in this thing, Captain?" Joey Knuckles shouted over the noise.

"She's been refitted with an aircraft engine, mates," he replied, firing high into the darkness behind them. "All me ships have. Ten miles out now."

The lights of the federal boats soon fell away in the distance. Recinella noticed that the cannon fire had ended. The crew were already cooling the guns down with sea water, securing the powder kegs. The engine hissed harshly behind them.

The captain stepped aside from the machine gun. "Let's get those sails stowed proper now," he called out. "What's that blasted racket?"

"Captain, best have a look," one of the men shouted from the bow, and he moved away to join him beside the rumbling motor.

Recinella looked about. The crew remained busy putting away all those sails, the captain hunched over, completely engrossed with whatever was wrong with the engine. Joey Knuckles stood awkwardly beside him, waiting.

It was the chance he'd been looking for.

The lower quarters would be empty. The captain's room unguarded. And, the chest.

Recinella moved quickly down the steps, past the other men too busy to notice as he stepped by. The room remained well lit, shadowed in its corners by the lanterns' light. He wasted no time and moved straight for the chest.

Gold. Bonds. A Mafia don's heart. It clearly held something important to the great sea captain.

He set the chest on the desk and his knife's blade made easy work of picking away its lock. He checked the door quickly, listened to the busy feet shuffling above deck. For a moment, it sounded as if someone was screaming. No matter.

The lid opened slowly, revealing its secret stash.

A book?

He picked up something called *The Count of Monte Cristo* by Alexandre Dumas, then another. One called *Twenty Thousand Leagues Under the Sea*.

The leather covers were worn, the pages aged. Beneath the first two books was another. It was titled *Treasure Island*, written by some guy named Stevenson.

Beneath were some photos. The faces somewhat familiar. Then, newspaper clippings. Chicago. The Falcone family. *He did kill him…* Recinella thought, confused.

It made no sense. Where was the money? Bonds? A treasure map, even. Some form of smoking gun?

He picked up *Treasure Island* again. It seemed the most worn and Recinella flipped through it.

He found writing in the front.

The inscription read simply: *"Merry Christmas, Sal. 25th December, 1887. With Love from your Uncle Giuseppe and Aunt Nancy. Sogni d'oro!"*

"Sweet dreams," he translated.

Sal, he thought. *Salvatore Falcone*.

The doorway opened then as the captain stepped into the doorway. His parrot fluttered its bright wings at his shoulder.

Recinella reached for his gun but found the chest holster empty. The captain held his .38 in the belt at his waist, beside his own ancient pistol. He was smiling. Recinella thought immediately of the photos he'd found in the chest. Familiar again.

Then he finally understood and the realization hit him harder than the cold ocean air blowing in through the opened doorway. "You didn't *kill* Falcone…," he said, and the book dropped lightly from his hands.

The dark figures of the crew hovered in the doorway just behind the hulking shape.

"You *are* Falcone," he finished.

The crew chuckled.

"Where's Joey?" Recinella asked. The words were half choked.

"Come now, Mr. Recinella," the pirate smiled, stepping fully into the room. "It's nigh time we showed ye 'bout walkin the plank."

"*Walkin' the plank,*" the parrot shrieked, "*Walkin' the plank!*"

NOTES: *American Prohibition, when the government deemed alcohol illegal, lasted from 1920 to 1933. During that time, perhaps predictably, liquor was smuggled into and throughout the States a hundred different ways, including by boat. Skilled seamen with the stomach for danger could make substantial livings supplying Caribbean rum, Canadian whiskey, French champagne, and English gin along the coasts and the Great Lakes. It wasn't long before organized crime became involved. Most sea smuggling occurred along the Rum Line, an imaginary line of U.S. jurisdiction twelve miles off the coast. Larger foreign ships loaded with alcohol would sit at the line, and there meet local fisherman and smaller boat captains who would, in turn, deliver the contraband to men waiting ashore, ready to deliver the liquor to secret speakeasies and bars throughout the States. Rum running and Prohibition ended together on December 5, 1933 with the passage of the 21st Amendment, repealing the ban. The busiest Rum Row was along the New Jersey coast, running between New York and Philadelphia, as more than fifty rum runners could be spotted on any given night. Often these ships sunk at sea or were forced to dump their cargo prior to government patrol boarding, and to this day, these same bottles, some still unbroken and unopened, will wash ashore to be found on Jersey beaches.*

THE SEA PROMISE

1968, DELAWARE

I've heard Some tell that the Devil knows many things because He is Old. I've also heard that he was once a ship's Captain. In either Case, then, listen to my Tale.

I was born Theodore Burke, the seventh Son of Thomas and Caroline Burke in Woolwich, where my Father was from a Line of Ship Builders and I learnt some of that Trade towards that same End. I soon came to Understand, however, that my Father had never once, in Thirty Tears, sailed on one of the Ships he'd helped build. All he had to Show for a Life of hard Work was a dirt-floort House in lower Woolwich and fourteen pitiable Children. I wanted more.

I'd heard yarns of the high Seas, of the Adventure and Fortune waiting there. Of Captains Ingemar and Drake. The golden Cities and strange Peoples of New Spain and the diamond Mines of the Dark Continent. At thirteen, I joined the Crew of a merchant ship and traveled twice to the New World. My unspoken Hope was to join a Privateer at first Chance, and the Great Author rewarded my secret Desire when our Ship was seized by Pirates off Hispaniola. It was then that I first took Service aboard the Theodosia under the Flag of Captain Marwood.

Piracy is oft called the "Sweet Trade" and I Confess that I rightly learnt why in those first Years. It was a fine Crew, an eager Crew, and the Spoils of our "Trade" were grand indeed. In a given

Month, I often held in my Hands more Money than me Father had made in ten Years. And, all we'd ever done to take it was scare a few Men. With Money, we had as much Rum and Wenches as we cared for and Taverns from Port Royal to Baltimore was fillt with our Banter, our Gaming, and our Brawls. Through all, we were as Free as the first golden Gods who'd walked the Earth. When the Money was Spent, as it often was within a Week, we simply sailed out for more. Though, at times, the Ship had no Food and we either slipped ashore to steal it from some Farmstead or made our Stew from the Rats caught below. Me best Mates during these Years was William Brill, Pepper, and James Hyde. We four eventually took a Ship of our own to Captain and they were exciting Times. Each Day brought some new Adventure or Mischief. In the Summer of '91, we capturt a Spanish Ship, The Atalaya off of Havana, and we made off with a Chest of Treasure that we Kept for ourselves. Seven hundred thousand Pesos. Jewels. Enough Pieces of eight to last a Lifetime. I now record Faithfully what became of said Chest and where Ye might find the Sum of our Full Fortune.

☠ ☠ ☠

The sailboat glided like a hungry shark along the shoreline. Four scouts were pressed against its railing, binoculars jammed to their eyes, standing tall, searching for the hidden inlet the pirate's letter had mentioned. The last boy, a boatswain named Chris Maher, manned the tiller from the cockpit and kept his eyes on the Atlantic, leery of hitting a sand bar this close to the beach as the waves broke starboard and the light tide pushed against their southward course.

Somewhere between Slaughter Beach and Broadkill, the irony of the names not lost on any of the boys, was where the pirate Burke had led them. There, he'd hinted from his 250-year-old grave, could be found a sliver of an entrance back up into the marshes, hardly noticeable unless there'd been good rain or a heavy sea storm. So, the boys had waited. The long spell of dry weather had given them plenty of time to study the letter, to review the old charts — and to plan what they might do with all the gold.

It was Chris who'd found the yellowed manuscript in his grandfather's barn, tucked into a squat chest, between a stack of old school primers and musty song books. The handwriting was scrawled with hundreds of loops and bizarre f's where s's should be, almost unreadable. He'd asked about the letter, asked where it had first come from, but his Grandma Mable had only waved him away, told him to take whatever he found.

He'd taken it straight to the others.

The crew of the *S.S.S. Fortune* included Yowler, Ross, Fielder, and Lundy. A group of five that'd sailed together for two years now, and surely his best pals outside of scouting too. He played fullback on the football team — the Milford Buccaneers no less — with two of them, and he and Yowler had talked for months about starting a band together. Something like The Doors or maybe even that new psychedelic English band Yowler was raving about, Pink Floyd. Just needed to save up a bit more to buy a full drum set. A lone used snare drum wasn't going to cut it. But, that wouldn't be a problem once the day was done. After all, they were on an actual treasure hunt.

They'd done some research, of course. Books in the library had confirmed that the *Atalaya* was a real ship in the Spanish fleet, and that a man named Marwood was hung for piracy in Yorktown in 1695, which made the rest of the note quite possible. Why else would this Burke character have given directions for them all to the end? He'd been imprisoned himself, no doubt. Scheduled for execution. It made sense. If he couldn't use it, maybe he wanted someone to have the treasure. A son, perhaps. Or even a great-great-great-great grandson who'd stumbled upon some strange family heirloom.

Chris looked back, the wooden lighthouse off Slaughter Beach lost around the bend. The ocean's waves capped and broke across the unspoiled coast and the shore's vegetation grew lush and green up to the water. Wide strands of salt marsh cordgrass, and eelgrass rustled behind hundreds of sandpipers who worked the high-tide line. He suddenly imagined Theodore Burke overlooking the same and found himself wondering what dreams and plans *he'd* had for the treasure.

165

"There!" Fielder shouted him back to reality. "Just right of the feeding frenzy."

Chris looked with the others, followed Fielder's excited pointing towards the small pack of scuttling gulls and terns gobbling the morning crabs. He lifted his own binoculars, found the spot between the tall grasses, the narrow opening hardly visible if you weren't looking for it.

"Do you really think that's it?"

"Might be."

Chris purposely let the wind spill from the ship's sails and slowed to get another look. "It could be it," he said.

"We really going back there?" asked Ross, and the others looked back to see what Chris thought.

He looked past them to the shore and considered the thick marsh grasses and dunes that stretched for miles. They'd told Mr. Bardo, their adult skipper, that they'd be bird watching, that they planned to have the boat back in just a few hours. But, this week's outing was secretly a bit more than sailing or advanced meteorology. "Sure we are," he said. "You think I came all the way out just to hang out with you dorks?"

Yowler belched in response.

"My point exactly," Chris smiled. "Get the anchor ready. Let's so find our treasure."

☠ ☠ ☠

The Floorboards of a Ship's Gundecks are usually painted Red so the Men won't lose Nerve when they see all the Blood once the Fighting starts. But, You still see it. You notice it when the Sea washes it across your Boots and froths pink over the Gunwales. In the late Summer that same year, our Ship was set upon by another Pirate Crew. 'Twas old Marwood himself, our old Captain. Seemed he'd gotten Word of our recent Catch and wanted a Look for Himself. It was a nasty Affair and many Hands was lost for both Crews. We carried eighteen working Cannon those Months.

Marwood had more and he'd loaded his with Grapeshot to Kill our Crew and Save the Ship. It was a red Morning for sure. Pepper was killed that Day.

We escaped, and the Ship limpt for Charlestown to make repairs. During those next Days, two of our own Crew attempted to take the Ship. They'd spoken of it, in any Case. They were Both draggt beneath the Keel for this until they was Dead. Made for the Chesapeake, but several British frigates chast Us off at the Mouth, and We turnt up along the Coast instead. They Pursued us and We set off in a smaller Ship, letting the rest of the Crew go. William and James argued a great Deal during this time. All matter of whether we should Forsake the Ship or where we should keep the Money. There were even accusations made that One or the Other had already lifted some from the Box. William said he knew a Point in Delaware, an Inlet we might get up in one of the Jolly Boats. There were many Turns as the Water branches off throughout the Marsh. A rolling Hitch is the key there. At the end of it, a high Bluff of solid Land, enough to build a Shelter to Hide from the Brits and Locals. We buried the Treasure there. Later that Night, William shot James.

☠☠☠

The rolling hitch, an all-purpose sailor's knot thousands of years old, appears on ships almost as much as sails themselves. Each of the boys had learned to tie the basic loop when they'd first joined the Sea Scouts and their understanding of Burke's clue, if it really was a clue, was immediate. Over to the right, looped back around twice to the left and then led right again through that last loop. Right, left, left, right.

They'd struggled through the first two turns already, moving ever deeper into the marshes while the burdened dinghy hit bottom and Yowler and Chris labored at the oars. At the second left, an hour into their adventure, they'd left the boat behind, dragging it onto a clump of eelgrass. Now, all five boys plodded grimly in the waist deep water, their blue pants soaked past the knees, faces red and dripping in the mid-morning sun. Chris took the white sailor's cap from his head and used it to wipe the salty sweat on his brow. While the pungent smell of the marsh grass assaulted his last nerve, he listened to the others slogging just behind him.

"Because a planet of talking apes is, um, completely moronic," Fielder replied. "Do I really need another reason?"

"Whatever," said Ross. "I just thought it was a pretty cool movie."

"*Bullitt's* a pretty cool movie, banana breath. We should all just go see that one again. Apes riding bikes and another Charlton Heston loincloth shot —That just ain't groovy."

"McQueen's boss," Yowler confirmed.

"Totally."

"They ride horses, by the way. The apes, I mean."

"Please stop talking."

"Or? "

"Or my sudden need to punch your face might not go away."

"How many times," Yowler goaded Fielder.

"Many. How much longer?"

"A left and a right, I guess."

Ahead of them, Chris shook his head. "We just took the second left, ladies."

"Oh, yeah."

"What if this doesn't lead anywhere? What if the big knot clue doesn't mean anything?" Ross pushed ahead some. "Or if they tied knots differently back then."

"Or —"Yowler tossed an arm around Fielder's shoulder, "— what if apes rode bikes?"

"Get away from me."

"Lundy, you wanna pick it up a bit pal. Hey, Lundy!"

"Don't chop on me, man," the boy grumbled back.

"Sounds like someone needs his nap."

Lundy lifted a finger over his shoulder. "Climb it, Tarzan."

"I guess we shouldn't chop on him, man."

Yowler groaned. "You really think we're gonna find all that gold?"

"Pesos are silver," Chris reminded again.

"No," Ross replied. "You see *Dark Shadows* yesterday?"

"Then, why we doing this?"

Fielder shrugged. "I don't watch that junk anymore. Barnabus was groovy for awhile, but I hated all that mad doctor crap and that Adam storyline. Lame. You wanna fight, Panty Waist?"

"Ain't there a merit badge for treasure hunting?"

"Barnabus was always lame." Chris added and pointed ahead. "There's our right."

"You think?"

"Has to be."

Chris had stopped and the others crowded around him looking up the narrow creek.

"Is that what I think it is?" Ross said.

Chris nodded. "A 'high bluff with solid land.'"

"Land ho, me hearties!" Yowler growled with one eye squinted closed. "It's bloody time to be gettin' our booty."

The boys laughed as one, forgetting the last two hours, and splashed from the creek up the hill.

☠ ☠ ☠

My Father once crafted a wind Chime from Scraps of different Woods he'd found at the Boatyard in Woolwich. After the Others went to Sleep, I watched Him by the lantern Light as he whittled and Shapt the Pieces, hollowed them to meet His exact Plan. It was a Gift for Mother, he said and smiled. She hung it from the front Door the next Morning and many Nights after, I went to Sleep to the gentle Sound of those Blocks clacking Together. I thought of that Chime while watching my old Crewmates hung at the Gallows in Dover. There were Five of different Shape and Length who droppt as one in a long Row. They'd been Caught outside of Canterbury

*and given a speedy Trial, while Marwood was sent to London for
a grander Investigation. McGrath, Pramp, and Vogt had Died right
away but the Last, Byrant and Samuel, still kicked and jerked on
their Lines like they was dancing a Jig. They twisted into the Others
and soon all Five swayt back and forth unevenly on the cold Breeze.
The Hangman climbt above Samuel and jumpt on both his Shoulders to finish the Job as old Sam had likely paid him to do had it
come to That. But, Bart struggled for many Minutes thereafter. I
have never been back to Woolwich.*

*After they was Hung, William and I went back to our Hide-
away in the Marsh and stayed low for many Months. She proved
cold and wretched but the Authorities was looking for us and there
was a reward offered too so we stayt there through most of that year.
We talked of stealing another ship and putting together another
Crew. Maybe heading back out to Sea. Shortly thereupon, William tried to kill me but his Pistol misfired. He'd never taken to the
Blade like I had. Anyhow, I helped William Understand he'd done
a Bad Thing that Night. Then, I gave him his Half and told him to
Depart. I ain't seen him since. You'll find my Share of this World in
a round Case in her Bonnet.*

☠ ☠ ☠

It had been more than an hour already, the top of the clearing pocked
with dozens of small shallow holes. "There's nothing here."

"What'd you expect, spaz? It's been like eight hundred years."

"Two hundred," Chris corrected. "Let's just keep digging. We're
bound to find nails or…" *The chimney.* Their belief was that, according to
their research, chimney caps were once called bonnets and that, since Burke
had called their hideaway "she," that "her bonnet" might mean a compartment hidden in the top of the smokestack.

"So," Ross rested his spade on his shoulder. "You guys seen a picture of that Olivia Hussey yet?"

"Who's that?"

"She's the fox playing Juliet in that new movie."

"I heard she's totally stacked."

Yowler lifted his hands dramatically to the blue sky above. "But, soft! What light through yonder sweater breaks?"

"Very nice," Chris chuckled, scooping away more dirt. "Will'd surely be touched."

"Heard she's also totally nude in a couple scenes."

"Shakespeare's a flippin' genius."

"You wanna go see it?"

"Are you insane? Ain't no sweater gonna get me to sit through all those stupid *thees* and *thous*. I'd rather watch talking apes."

"Hey," Lundy called out on his knees, "I hate to interrupt your gripping conversation, but, I got something over here." He lifted the large stone out of the ground and wiped it off on his dark blue pants.

"So what?" Fielder said. "It's a rock."

"So, there's a bunch of 'em." He looked up at the others. "And they're all this big."

The digging for the next half hour was done quietly and with genuine exertion. It was no different than when the same group had worked on celestial navigation badge together or taken their first night cruise in heavy weather. They dug out in both directions, following the trail of stones as if a chimney had collapsed a hundred years before.

When they found the small round metal box between several of the stones, there were no screams of celebration. Only shocked silence. It proved to be the first time any of them had really thought of the hunt as real. Until that moment, it had all just been a game. Something fun to do together. Now, it took on a different feel altogether, and not an entirely welcome one.

The small box was badly rusted through, ginger-black holes rotted at its corners and underneath. Chris lifted it out carefully and laid it on the ground. "It's heavy," he said.

For awhile, they simply stared at it.

"It's too small for all that gold."

Fielder shrugged. "Could be the jewels only. Maybe we just need to keep digging for the gold."

"Go ahead, Chris," Yowler nudged him. "Open it."

Chris slowly grabbed hold of the cold box from the top but found the lid was rusted stuck. He tapped it lightly with the side of his spade, then lifted the lid slowly from both sides, the top lifting off completely like the lid of a hatbox. The others leaned in for a better look.

"What is it?"

Chris lifted the contents out from the box. "It's paper," he said. "Old paper, I think. It's. . . " He held up the brown glop. Sodden and rotted, the ancient parchment fell thru his hand and back into the ancient container. "It's nothing. These pages are ruined."

"Then where's the stinking treasure?" fumed Ross. "Is that money?"

"Yeah," Fielder's face was balled in confusion. "Where's all the gold?"

"Silver," Chris said. "I don't think there is any."

"Then, maybe the note's the treasure," Fiedler pressed. "Maybe it's just another clue."

"Maybe," Chris thought. "But, not in the way you mean. "

"We'd better keep digging," Ross said.

"No," Chris stood, leaving the box where it was. "There's nothing else here."

"But, he said — "

Chris reached down to place the lid back over the rusted box. "He promised only the 'sum of their fortune.'"

"So?'

"So —" Chris looked about the empty clearing, then turned back around to the others. "— I think that's what we got."

"A rotted-out shack in the middle of a swamp."

"Yeah," Chris smiled. "I think so."

"That, ah," Fielder thought for the right words, "that sucks."

"Yeah," Chris said. "I guess so."

"So now what?" Yowler said.

Chris shook his head. "I guess we're done here."

"But —" Fielder stammered. "— Oh, hell. I'm starving anyway. You guys wanna split a pizza when we get back?"

"Done," Yowler stood with the others and started moving down from the clearing. Chris hung back just a minute more, a strange feeling tightening his throat.

"That was kinda cool," Ross said as he moved past him.

"Yeah."

Chris looked over the clearing again, listened to the lonely rustle of the tall marsh grass that surrounded them. He'd wondered before what Burke had felt along these same waters, what thoughts had raced through his mind when he overlooked the same shore. Now, Chris had an idea.

"Hey, Captain Ahab, you comin' or what?" one of the boys shouted back to him.

Chris waved and walked down the hill towards his waiting friends, then the five boys headed for the boat together.

☠ ☠ ☠

If you're reading this, I have taken You as far as I might and You've Found all that's left of my Years at Sea. There's little more to Tell. William returnt one Night when I was gone to Town and Took the rest of the Money. I heard later that He was hung in Norfolk for Murder. Except for some Day work on the Crab boats, I've spent the better part of the last twenty Years now here, in this Hideaway. The Locals suspected me for my Past, I heard their Whispers of "Murderer" — "Villain." They saw the Stain upon me clearly. While Many Pirates has Gone on to become Gentlemen of power in Government or Commerce, most was that before they started. I was only the Son of Thomas Burke, Shipbuilder. Had I but known, then, that was Treasure enough.

NOTES: *Sea Scouts (A division of the Boy Scouts of America) is a world-wide organization and home to some seven thousand U.S. boys and girls between the ages of 14 and 21. While predominantly found along our coasts, Sea Scouts exist throughout the entire country, also sailing local lakes and rivers. The group was founded by Royal Navy Admiral Warrington Baden-Powell, brother of Boy Scouts founder Thomas Baden-Powell and, like regular Scouts, it includes a series of ranks and merit awards directly related to seamanship. At its peak, just before World War II, there were 27,000 Sea Scouts in the U.S. The Navy, who actively recruited former Sea Scouts following Pearl Harbor, claimed the program proved a vital role in America's swift readiness when entering the war. After a significant decline in the 1970s, the program is again, today, one of the fastest growing segments in scouting.*

FIDDLER'S GREEN

2006, MARYLAND

September 4 (Ocean City) — *The search for missing diver,*
Michael Waldon, 42, will continue along the northern Assateague
Island shoreline today, as the seas are again expected to be too rough
for divers, according to sheriff's deputy Alex Donne. Seven divers on
Wednesday found no sign of Waldon, who disappeared while wreck
diving between Ocean City and the Assateague State Park. Waldon
was reported missing by authorities on Saturday when his deserted
boat was discovered anchored in the area. The U.S. Coast Guard
gave up its search on Tuesday but Worcester County authorities have
been searching since. Waldon disappeared in fifty feet of water one
half mile off the Sinepuxent Bay Wildlife Management area, Donne
said. Donne said Waldon's airtank was found and the operation is
now considered a recovery effort. Waldon was a visiting professor of
English at the University of Maryland and author of several books
of poetry, including The Caravan Passes, *which was the 1991*
winner of the prominent Morrow-King Poetry Award, a college
spokeswoman said.

"Ahoy, mate!"

Michael snapped out of his strange daydream and shielded his eyes from the midday sun to look out towards the approaching vessel. A twenty-foot, single-masted Coronado with its sails down, engine purring, came in just behind his diving flag. At the tiller sat its only crew, an older man hunched against the bitter September winds.

"Ahoy," Michael hailed back, waving a hand, pleased to use the time-honored greeting, as corny as it sounded. He wondered where the man had come from, he'd been out of the water for awhile and hadn't noticed him before, and welcomed the passing company. It'd been a strange morning and he'd felt out of sorts with the world. A quick visit with a fellow boater might get him back in the swing of things.

The other boat had slowed its engine to pull alongside and now drifted easily in the ocean's lifting swells. "Rough day for diving, ain't it?" the man called through cupped hands.

Michael glanced up at the sky. "Only gonna get worse later."

The old man followed the look, shook his head in agreement. "Right you are, lad." He turned back to Michael, nodded at the ocean's dark water. "'Aving any luck?"

"Just swimming about, really. Some good-sized fish out this way."

"Sure, sure there are," the man said and something in his voice heralded the next words. "But you're not really looking for fish, are you?"

Michael laughed, feigning confusion. "What do you mean?"

"You're looking for the *Geraldine*, naturally."

Michael studied the old man's face and met eyes as sharp and blue as the ocean. He thought immediately of Hemingway's Santiago. Cheerful and undefeated. The face was browned by years in the sun and as weather-worn as the small sailboat. "Yeah," Michael admitted. "I'd heard there might be a wreck out this way. Clearly not the first to look, huh?"

"No. But not too many head this far north," the man looked out over the ocean. "Most stick closer to the bay."

"Why's that?" He knew the answer of course; he had studied the history of the *Geraldine* for six months, but was curious what the old man knew.

"Folks in Spence say they saw her sink, I guess. And, the gold coins."

"Still wash ashore off Chincoteague Bay they told me."

"Not since '78."

"When'd she sink?"

The old man squinted at him and Michael knew he'd been caught playing dumb. "'85," the old sailor said evenly.

"1685. Amazing. You local?"

"Not really."

Michael waited for more, but nothing else came from the old man, who simply sat staring out at the ocean. Michael wondered, then, if he were talking with another scavenger, the all-too-common treasure vultures who somehow always managed to appear around the legitimate hunters and dives. Where genuine hunters put in months, or even years, hitting the books and flipping through dusty manuscripts, letters, and court documents before stepping onto a boat or beach, the weekend scavengers were quick to appear when word of a successful professional expedition had spread. The old man's sails were covered, too. He'd come out for more than a pleasure cruise.

"Well," Michael said. "I'd better get going. Hoping to get another dive in before it gets too dark." He patted his BCD vest to help conclude the conversation, remembering he needed to swap out his regulator. The demand valve was all out of whack, had been since the first dive of the day. He waved and turned back towards his equipment. "Enjoy the rest of your day."

"'Ow'd you like to dive the *Geraldine*?" The voice came over the wind between them.

Michael turned slowly. "Sorry?"

"I've got a pretty good idea where she lies."

Sure you do, Michael thought. "That's okay," he smiled. "The fish are fine by me. Think I may have found some of a 1940's wreck just below anyway."

"They say Captain Gates had a girl up in Bishopville."

Michael froze. It was one of his main theories that the ship's captain, Bartholemy Gates, had pushed the *Geraldine* too hard its fateful night to get closer to home, that he'd fought out of the Sinepuxent inlet and headed north against the storm. He'd even read one of the letters between the two lovers. It'd been used as evidence against one of his crew by the records of the Admiralty. "Yes," he said. "Rebecca."

The old man's face broke into a wide, crinkled smile. His boat purred alongside Michael's. "That's right. So how come all that gold was found in the inlet?"

"The ship was too heavy. Gates jettisoned everything he could, including some of the prize. There was enough to dump."

"Delgado's manifest said Gates had 30,000 gold doubloons stolen from him."

"Delgado's an infamous liar. It was likely more than twice that. The rest for himself and his men when they returned to Spain. Alas, Gates and his crew took it all." Michael looked along the coast. "Until the *Geraldine* went down in a storm in August of '85."

The old man nodded. "Seventy-four men drowned. Four survivors."

"One of them an eighteen-year-old boy named McDonough who estimated 60,000 doubloons and another 50,000 ounces of virgin silver were aboard the ship."

"Just before he got hung for piracy."

"Right. So take away the few hundred doubloons that have washed ashore over the last three hundred years and —"

"Leaves quite a bit more still to be found, doesn't it?" The man pointed a bony finger.

"I never do it for the gold."

"Neither did I, lad. Neither did I."

Michael felt the smile form across his own face, welcomed it. "But, it's a nice perk, isn't it?"

"That it is," the old man nodded. "Permission to come aboard, Capt'n?"

"Permission granted," Michael said.

They'd moved the boats several miles north of Ocean City just outside Assawoman Bay and had anchored in about seventy feet of dark water, bobbing in the deep swells. By then, they'd lashed the old man's sail boat against Michael's dive boat and brought him aboard, and Michael'd learned that the stranger's name was Bart and that just beneath them, half buried in silt and sand, was *something*.

Whether or not it was truly the *Geraldine* remained to be seen, and it seemed unrealistic. There were hundreds of wrecks along the eastern coast, most nothing more than rotted-out merchant vessels torpedoed in the world wars. In fact, Michael had been swimming about one just before Bart showed. A tricky dive, shifting currents of three or four knots churning below. Lost control. Things got confused for a bit. Dark. Then the problems with his regulator and tank had forced him up and out of the water.

But that was all a foggy memory now. Now, he was focused on Bart and his story of a pirate captain who'd mistakenly feared the bay as a death-trap and sought safety further up the coast. Bart showed him an older chart where there'd once been a small creek that came off Assawoman Bay. It would have provided safe harbor had they made it, a creek the British Navy had used before. And, Gates had begun his career as a marine with the fleet.

Bart's story was already half-confirmed by the boat's sonar. Something significant was down there. After all, there are few circles and no straight lines in nature. But, what?

By the time they'd found the spot, it was too late for a dive. The sun had dipped over the natural dunes an hour before, the clouds above lined arterial red. Too late for a safe dive, at any rate. It had been a long day already and Michael felt tired, out of it, as it was. If it truly was the *Geraldine*, it had rested on the Atlantic's floor for some three hundred years. It could wait until morning.

"Delgado's report to Garza claimed he'd fired at the pirates before they boarded." Michael had refilled the cup with coffee and some whiskey and stepped back on deck to hand it back to the older man sitting in the cockpit.

"Thank you, lad. Almost as good as the brew at the *Canes Venatici*." He winked. "A little tavern in town me and the mates been known to gather at.

So, what do you think of Delgado's report?"

"*Canes Venatici*. The stars, yes? The 'Hunting Wolves.' I think Delgado would have been hacked to pieces if he'd so much as risen his voice that morning." Michael sat in the seat opposite the old man, stretched out his legs along the bench. "More likely, he fired a few cursory shots *after* the pirate crew was finished. The *Geraldine* may have taken a shot then."

"Aye."

"Low on the hull, below the waterline. Most likely fothered the hole with a shredded sail to seal it up, and that worked as far as Maryland. But the storm proved too much. Probably should have stopped to fix it."

"Why didn't they, do you suppose?"

"Just ready to get home, I'd say. From McDonough's testimony, it looks as if they'd been out to sea eight months at that point. Seems a lot of the men had established roots down here. There are church records that suggest Gabe Braker, one of the crew, was married at the Presbyterian church in Pocomoke City. Another, Harrison or Hamberson, not sure, was born over in Crisfield."

"You've studied well, lad."

"You're the one that got us here, mystery man. Dropping out of thin air. Seems I'm not the only one who's done his homework. You've clearly found some brilliant source material yourself."

The man only nodded.

"Interesting times," Michael mused, looking over his boots to watch where the rolling black of the ocean now met the stable ebony of the sky. "Interesting men."

"They was indeed," Bart blew a ring of smoke from his pipe. "Most now gone to Davy Jones's Locker or the Green."

Michael sipped his coffee. "Fiddler's Green?"

"Aye. You've heard of it?"

"Sure. Some kind of sailor heaven, right? I know Jones's Locker is the resting place of drowned seamen."

"Most of 'em. The men also spoke of Fiddler's Green as the place where fittin' sailors go."

"Fitting?"

"True men of the sea. Adventurers and noble rogues. Men of real spirit. Proper sailors and pirates, ye might say. When they was killed or Time finally chased 'em down."

"And for these few, a celestial paradise. An eternal celebration and supply of life's essentials: booze, tobacco, and equally spirited women."

Bart grinned, lifted his coffee. "Where the mugs and pockets is never emptied."

Michael smiled back and the two fell into silence for some time, simply enjoying the sound of the churning wind and the waves lapping against the boat, the wind against their faces.

"Quite the arm ye got there," Bart said suddenly.

"Oh." Michael leaned up. "This? Yeah." He studied the man, found it odd he'd mentioned his prosthetic arm. He'd worn various models over the years, the latest a dynamic prostheses that started just above his elbow and used sophisticated myoelectrics to read the tenses of his remaining arm muscle to transmit signals to the artificial hand. Most folk tended to keep away from the issue altogether.

"What 'appened?"

"Remnants of youth. Wakeboarding down in Tennessee with my cousins. Seventeen, I guess. Trying a new move and the cord and handle wrapped up my arm funny. Cut the bicep in half and slashed the brachial artery. Doctor couldn't save it."

"Doctors weren't never any good. Better chance surviving direct cannon fire than any respectable sawbone's blade. You're not from Tennessee, though."

"No. Michigan. Worked my way around a bit. Philly. Charleston, taught at the college. Mexico for a spell."

"And now Maryland."

"Just for the year. Teaching a couple courses up at the university." Bart nodded his head, but Michael suddenly had the suspicion the old man had never heard of the school. "School's too big for my taste, but it was a nice opportunity to search for the *Geraldine*."

"Not your first dive for gold." Like most of the old man's comments, it was said as a statement, not a question.

"No. There was a small Dutch sloop off Connecticut. And, the *Ambrose*, an English privateer off Barbuda."

"I always liked Barbuda."

Michael was glad the man hadn't followed up with any questions about what exactly he'd found in those dives or how much. Most people did, and it often proved awkward. It had been sizable, enough to live pretty comfortably and finance another four years of traveling and wreck dives in spots such as Belize, Vigo Bay, and Hatteras. "A fellow traveler, I see," Michael said. "Couldn't quite place the accent."

"Sailed the whole world, I did." Bart chuckled. "Born in Brighton. Then worked the Middle Passage a bit. African Coast. Boston. The West Indies. Here in Maryland a spell." Michael wondered what he'd meant by the Middle Passage, thought only of the slave trade. "Always loved the freedom and infinite possibility of a strong wind in the sails." He looked out over the black water. "Like you, it seems."

"Well, I tried the other way." Michael smiled. "I really did. Right out of college, worked almost ten years writing TV commercials and junk mail, working up the ladder, for a couple agencies in Philadelphia. Eventually realized I spent most of my time sitting in meetings whose outcomes didn't really matter. The rest of the day was typing emails to people whose primary interest was protecting pointless jobs they hated anyway." He shook his head and finished his coffee. "Guess I never learned to play by the rules."

"Some don't, thank the stars. So, ye turned to the sea."

"*Over the glad waters of the dark blue sea, our thoughts as boundless, and our souls as free. Far as the breeze can bear...* I'd sailed the Great Lakes as a kid. Always — Well, bought the boat with the prize money from some silly poetry thing. Made the travel easy."

"What about a lass?"

Michael laughed, thought for a moment. "That didn't work out either I guess." He could tell Bart was waiting for more. "We had love, but she wanted a husband even more. And, that just wasn't something I could do for

182

her." He chuckled, moving towards the bow and grabbing hold of the railing to collect himself. "I may have over-spiked my coffee, Bart. I've gone chatty tonight. Head filled with memories, strange thoughts."

"You want to do this now?" Bart asked behind him.

Michael looked into the black water, watched its roll, and imagined the blacker world waiting just beneath. The prize within. "Yeah," he said. "I do."

☠ ☠ ☠

He dropped straight towards the wreck, moving through the dark water as if he were floating in the same weightlessness of space. His 15-watt halogen lamp blasted light below, chasing away the skulking darkness and he swallowed hard to clear the pressure increasing in his eardrums. The air in his mouth tasted like rubber. He recalled the unique taste of Nixodie, something wrong with the mixture on a previous dive. The current jumping to three or four knots, pinning him against the back of the wreck. Though the wet suit held back the cold, he imagined it passing through his body.

At fifty feet deep, the shapes below came into view through his half-misted mask. Though three hundred years had rotted away the hull and deck houses, collapsed the bow and stern, the cannons and anchors remained beside a familiar sequence of swollen lumps where the boat had fallen apart. He found the line of a stern, garlanded with seaweed and encrusted in lime beside the snow-white evidence of sunken lead. The light passed over unnatural coloring along the ocean floor where the cannons or anchors, deeply buried, had discolored the vegetation with the recognizable iodine stain of iron.

It was the *Geraldine* after all.

Michael kicked his fins, moved towards one of the buried lumps which shouted the hidden shape of a cannon that only a pro wreck diver would notice. He pulled the short pick from his belt and knocked away the sand, his feet kicking to hold his body vertical above the dig as the current pulled him towards the surrounding darkness.

The sand clouded around him, then quickly dissolved into the ocean. Abruptly, the cannon revealed itself. Iron cast, a fourteen pounder. He cleared away more, read its serial numbers. A2030. The Chamber of Amsterdam and the Dutch East India Company. Captain Gates had captured several Dutch ships in the 1640s. He wondered what action the cannon had ever seen, what sea battles it might whisper to him, then moved along the semiordered line of sand-covered lumps towards the stern. The collapsed gundeck was long since gone, the dozen cannons falling as one to the ocean floor, leading a loose trail away from where the quarterdeck and main cabin would have been.

The treasure was elsewhere. Bart had suggested it would be towards the bow. That Captain Gates had moved it, hidden it, among the salted pork barrels in the forward lower berths.

The old hunter had taken him this far, there was no reason to stop following his lead now.

Michael kicked over the rest of the ship, passing the familiar shape of buried anchors and decayed mollusk-covered decking. A large wahoo moved by lazily in the lamp's light, the prehistoric-looking fish seemingly uninterested by the intrusion. More straight lines and squares, overgrown with seaweed. A brass bell, tarnished and half lost in a growth of rock. Easy enough to chisel out later. Towards the bow now, he slowed and studied the darkness encroaching around him.

Something wasn't right.

A strange chill raced up his spine. The darkness pressed against the blaring light, pushing in like a living thing. He thought of it suddenly as an actual being, a presence, that wanted to take him. He'd fought away sharks in Barbuda and a ten-foot moray eel once, but this was something else. This predator could not be chased away. For the first time diving, ever, he was afraid.

Pushing through the odd clamor of anxiety, Michael began digging with his pick. Despite the darkness swirling about him, he felt a sudden warmth and optimism. He dug with purpose, his hand now moving with swift certainty, as if reclaiming a memory.

The pick hit something metallic. Broke through the top layer of the ocean's crust and calcified wood. He struck again, scraping the remaining sand and vegetation away. He'd expected the telltale olive glow that typically announced corroded coins. But the first coin was unspoiled gold, bright and glowing in his light.

Michael's heart pounded with excitement, and he could almost hear the heartbeat filling his ears above his own thunderous breath. He'd really found it. He chopped away more of the ocean, three hundred years of decay and life that had grown over the presumptuous piles of gold. The crates themselves had long since rotted away. Now, only the treasure remained.

Michael thought of Bart above and realized suddenly that the old man wouldn't be so surprised. The treasure was merely where he'd always thought it had been.

He holstered the pick and reached both hands into the pile of coins. The hand lamp faltered then, flickered its light across the ocean floor. The darkness moved in the spaces between, returning to press against him, crowding him. He shook the lamp and the light now gave out totally. Michael floated briefly in complete blackness, entirely weightless and without form. It was if he'd simply become one with the nothing which surrounded him.

Just beneath, however, the treasure's yellow glow slowly spread over his body, somehow filled the ocean with golden light. It was as if the sun were rising over some sea's black horizon. His eyes squinted against the glow and the light seemed to seep through him filling him with —

It lasted only a moment.

Then, the ocean's darkness swallowed him completely.

☠ ☠ ☠

Michael finished lashing his boat to the piling and stood alone on the dock to look over the vast ocean. The water was peculiarly blue and clear, calm, only the smallest promise of whitecaps across the rolls as a strong wind gusted across the waves. The dark silhouettes of ships sailed in the distance backed by a sky strangely tinted purple. The plump white clouds floating just above the boats' shapes looked gilded in gold.

He had never been to this dock before, did not recognize it, or even remember approaching it, delirious as he was by the time he'd returned to his boat. He didn't care where he was, though. All sailors eventually had to come ashore.

Other boats were housed across the docks and he walked past them towards the shore. Vessels of every imaginable shape. Sloops, crumsters and small schooners. Elaborate figureheads of beautiful women and greek gods. A World War II patrol boat, a Higgins he thought, with PT200 painted along its side. A frigate that looked as if it had sailed right off the pages of *Treasure Island* or *Hornblower*. As he passed, Michael imagined he'd even seen cannons along its lower decks. The docks remained empty.

He stood alone for some time, staring up the road away from the docks towards town. The ocean's cool wind cradled his tall form, pushed the long hair in his face. Up the hill, the faint glow of lights and life.

He started up the cobblestoned road towards it.

He'd walked a mile, he thought. Maybe more. Somehow, he felt as if he'd been walking all day and for only a few minutes at the same time. The town was typical of a hundred harbor towns he'd visited over the years. Squat buildings, weathered and timeless, peppered across a tall hill and grouped around a center square. Sagging gambrel roofs and peaked gables, a few Georgians with cupolas and railed widow's walks. Smoke lifted from dozens of chimneys, the sound of music and laughter drifting down the long road towards him. Still, no sign of another person.

The streets were lined in cobblestone, the various shops and houses pressed close together like young lovers. Dingy signs and lampposts dotted every other building. It was a town that had grown up unplanned, grown naturally around itself as needed over time. He wandered through the streets as if walking in a dream, not really sure of where he was going. He felt peculiar. Lost.

He wondered where the people were. Heard them somehow from a distance, but none of the taverns seemed right. He moved forward through the empty streets, deeply breathing the ocean's cool salty air with each step.

Then, he saw it. A shabby wooden sign swinging over one of the taverns. The intense profile of a wolf's head, strong and eager. Hungry for life. The *Canes Venatici*. The name seemed somewhat familiar, but he couldn't quite place it.

Yet, he moved towards it and opened the door.

Inside, the tavern was full. Men, sailors all by their dress and manner, hovered about the tables together. Drinking, joking, playing cards. Women moved about the room too, several sitting on laps and laughing the way only lively women can, one beautiful lass singing a tender melody from atop her table, accompanied by a lone dark-skinned fiddler.

At a table in the back, a familiar face sat surrounded by a mixture of chuckling sailing men as they listened to one of their own. Mugs sat before each as the man held out his arms in support of his tale. Between their laughter, Bart caught Michael's eye.

Bart. Bartholemay, Michael realized with a start. Bartholemay Gates.

"Ahoy, mate!" the pirate captain shouted over the crowd's revelry, and waved him over.

Michael waved back hesitantly, smiled, then stepped into the room to join them at last.

NOTES: *To reach the mystical land of Fiddler's Green, old sailors were told to walk inland with an oar over their shoulder until they reached a small village where people asked what they were carrying. Then, they would know they'd found Fiddlers Green. The legend likely owes some credit to Homer's* Odyssey, *where Odysseus is told that the only way to appease the sea god Poseidon and find happiness is to take an oar and walk until he finds a land where he is asked what he is carrying, and there make his sacrifice. As to the mystical name itself, there were real 17th-century village greens in such places as Wapping (East London), Portsmouth Point, and other port towns across England where sailors could spend their recent earnings on life's essentials: brew, tobacco and spirited women. Street-musician fiddlers gathered about these same village greens and the surrounding taverns and brothels, where their playing provided an agreeable ambiance for the sailors as they enjoyed themselves inside.*

THE LAST PIRATE

1718, NORTH CAROLINA

The children were screaming. *His* children. Sawyer and Murray. Their tiny voices, pitched high in terror, suddenly filled the dark home.

Keegan Sinclair spilled from his bed, throwing the blankets aside. His wife, Genny, gasped awake and sat up wide-eyed. "*What*," she blurted crossly. "What is it?"

Sinclair held out a hand to stay her questions, and fought to wake. He fumbled for his musketoon, his boarding pistol, but could not find it. No matter. He raced towards his sons.

The hall stretched somehow into the night and the boys' voices became more piercing and frantic. He staggered forward, the confusion of the suddenly unfamiliar passage falling away in shadow. Sinclair drew his cutlass from the scabbard at his hip and burst at last through the door.

In window-framed moonlight, the two boys huddled together in the far corner of the small room. They were crying, and their eyes were wide with fear. A massive black shape, larger than any man, loomed over them, blocking most of Sinclair's view. It carried an enormous boarding axe in its hairy hand, the blade tilted toward the boys. The thing turned slowly to reveal its demon face, the very flames of Hell flickering across the dark features. Smoke curled over snarling jaws and its eyes shined black in the darkness like a shark's eyes, unfeeling and hungry. It drew a long cutlass with its other hand and charged forward. Sinclair —

Sinclair woke with a choked scream. In the darkness, his hammock rocked uneasily, and he grabbed the beam inches above to steady himself. Though he recognized quickly it wasn't his usual ship, the familiar din of creaking boards and clattering rigging soon supplanted the nightmare's horror. He welcomed the sound of men snoring and the muffled hum of active voices on the upper decks. The dream's sinister images lingered though as he shook himself awake and wiped the sweat from his forehead.

Blackbeard. Likely the most feared pirate in the history of man, and, purportedly, the very spawn of the devil himself. Sinclair'd known the nickname alone to make women pale. The villain's escapades and savageness were notorious, and he'd quickly become the stuff of legend. The stuff of nightmares too, Sinclair supposed. A genuine *monster*.

And, they were hunting it.

Sinclair climbed out from the hammock and looked over the crowded space. A handful of sailors also lay sleeping, cocooned in the lower bunks. Sinclair at last noticed one of the other men was awake and watching him. He imagined the talk already. Sinclair, "Highlander," as many of the men called him, was behaving as a bloody child. He thought briefly of explaining himself, perhaps laughing off the incident. Instead, he simply cleared his throat as if to dismiss the matter, donned his light blue ensign's jacket, and made for the hatchway.

"Mr. Sinclair," one of the sailors greeted as he stepped on deck. "'Eren't expecting you for another two bells yet."

"Where are we?" Sinclair asked. The November winds felt cool across his face, the orange sun just now setting behind the scrub-lined sand dunes.

"Don't rightly know, sir. Just more of Nor' Carolina, I reckon'."

More of North Carolina. The two ships in the wretched convoy had been searching her shores for a week now. It was believed that Blackbeard was there, somewhere along the coast. On a tip from a passing merchant ship, they'd spent the previous day and night searching the length of Brant's Shoals off Roanoke. Allegedly, the pirate was grounded somewhere within, but they'd found nothing.

Not that anyone living in North Carolina particularly cared if they were successful. In fact, Sinclair thought, shaking his head, the opposite likely held true. Merchants from Bath to Charles Town had purchased cheap stolen goods from the pirate for years. Hell, the Governor himself, the "Honorable" Charles Eden, was a known supporter. He'd often given Blackbeard, and his men, safe refuge within the colony's borders, offering quick cursory pardons that were broken as soon as the pirate had finished cleaning his boats, rested a bit, and was ready to set sail again. Eden had even presided at the villain's last marriage. In return for those favors, who really knew. But, more than one servant had seen bags of *something* being carried into the Governor's mansion by Blackbeard's own men.

Sinclair looked towards the small quarterdeck of the *Jane* where Lieutenant Maynard hovered behind a small group of seamen, his hands behind his back, his lower lip scrunched over the upper in a permanent scowl designed to display sincere contemplation and interest. Sinclair suspected his commander incapable of either. With an unimposing career largely built on handshakes and connections, Sinclair figured that Maynard knew only as much about sailing and warfare as was necessary for polite conversations over dinner or a good game of whist. Still, as he approached, Sinclair gave the expected nod to his commander.

"Nice of you to join us, Mr. Sinclair," Maynard remarked.

Sinclair, who had slept all of five hours in the past two days, managed a curt "Yes, sir" and joined the others.

"Ocracoke, sir," Williams pointed to the chart. "There've been rumors that 'e planned to fortify the whole damn island."

Sinclair studied it, shook his head. "Naturally," he smiled. Blackbeard *would* be so bold.

"Could be buried in one of these inlets, sir. If —"

"Deeper waters, Mr. Williams," Maynard offered from behind them. "Best look east. That merchant captain sent us on a fool's errand, wouldn't you say, Mr. Sinclair? Undoubtedly, the scoundrel has learned of our approach and fled to sea."

Not bloody likely. Sinclair suppressed a smirk, suspected the other men were doing the same, as he glanced towards the *Ranger*, the other sloop running just behind them off port. While they'd managed to find sixty men to throw aboard the two leased ships, neither the *Jane* nor the *Ranger* carried artillery. Not a single cannon between them! In contrast, Blackbeard's infamous flagship carried forty guns and had recently defeated a British man-of-war on the open sea.

While Governor Spotswood of Virginia had certainly put his own money into the venture, Sinclair knew it was not enough. Only enough for Spotswood to loudly announce he'd ordered two teams to hunt down the Atlantic's most feared pirate. Enough, perhaps, to help the public forget the current political scandal — a trivial slight to the King's *birthday* no less, which Spotswood hadn't even made himself — that political enemies and the press had ignited into a full blown firestorm that'd plagued the Virginian governor and his council for months.

"Perhaps the merchant simply misjudged the actual location," Sinclair offered. "He seemed a reasonable fellow and quite sure of seeing the *Adventure* hidden out this way. To come upon Teach while he was stranded is the advantage we'll need to even things —"

Williams's shoulders had dropped some, and Sinclair felt his argument droop with them. The marine had apparently just decided it wasn't worth it to contradict his commander. What did he care if they found Blackbeard? There'd been no bonus offered the men over their usual wages. And, the pirate was an extraordinary killer. He could not fault William's reaction. "Come about seaward, sir?" Williams asked Maynard. "On what bearing?" The local pilot, the only one who'd agreed to join them, waited at the helm anticipating directions.

"Patience, patience," Maynard held out his hands now, "We should, I think, perhaps, first consider the possible escape routes that Mr. Teach and his crew might have followed. This is an important affair, Williams. Best not rush into such matters."

Williams sighed as more charts were tossed across the stand, then caught himself. "Sorry, sir," he apologized quickly to Sinclair. Other than

Maynard, Sinclair was the only other officer on the mission.

"It's been a challenging two days," Sinclair dismissed the slip and grabbed the chart "Let's take a look."

Under Maynard's stare, they'd gone over the charts for only a few minutes when a call came down from the mizzen top. "Mast, ho," the lookout waved his hands, then pointed. "Southwest. Mast, ho!"

The whole group followed the lookout's pointing over the high sand dunes. Maynard called for his telescope and Sinclair drew out his own short scope, a Christmas gift from Genny and the boys, to bring to his eye. He scanned over the shrubs and dune, imagining the inlet hidden just behind.

Sure enough, the thin black splinter of a mast now appeared in the scope's close-fitting sight, the very top of the masthead backlit in the setting sun. It appeared straight, no evidence of its grounding. But, thankfully, there was no lookout staring right back at them. Aground or not, *Blackbeard was caught unawares!*

"By God," Maynard gasped behind them, looking through his glass. "It's him."

Sinclair lowered his scope and turned with the others to await Maynard's next command. "Exact location, Mr. Williams?" Maynard asked.

"That's Beaufort Inlet," the helmsman said. "Tight shoal back there, even *with* the tide. No wonder the devil got stuck."

Williams had already found it on the charts. "Runs back far enough, sir. But, there's nowhere for 'im to go."

Sinclair took a look at the map. He imagined it best to strike quickly, before their own ships were spotted. A cutting-out party of some fifty men who could quietly row a half dozen launches up the inlet under the mask of dark. Or, perhaps, Maynard would order them to shore now, to carry the smaller boats *over* the dunes and reset them closer in. Either way, he imagined a small recon ship of a few would set out immediately to gather Blackbeard's exact condition. Sinclair also expected Maynard to choose him for the task and was glad of it. It had been too long waiting aboard the ship doing nothing. He was relieved to finally be doing something, and he felt that same energy move across the rest of the men.

It was almost ideal. Sinclair grinned. The surprise would be enough to neutralize the pirate's unmistakable artillery advantage. In daylight, their sixty muskets were no match against even five cannons. Under the cover of night, however, it was quite possible they could storm the ship.

Maynard had stepped forward to join them over the charts. "We have him bottled in," he said, studying the map. "He shan't escape this time."

"Shall I assemble the open boat crews, sir?" Sinclair asked, his stomach suddenly nervous about the way Maynard's eyes moved over the chart.

"We'll wait," Maynard said.

"Wait, sir?" Williams gasped before Sinclair could.

"Until morning," Maynard cleared his throat. "It's too dark now. We're just as likely to become as grounded as he apparently was."

"Not the smaller boats, sir." Sinclair pressed his luck.

"We'll take in both sloops, tomorrow morning, Mr. Sinclair. Press his back right against the wall." He tapped his finger on the chart. One of the sailors openly groaned, but Maynard pretended he hadn't heard it.

"Sir, might I – " Sinclair indicated that they should speak in private, but Maynard held his position, bringing his hands behind his back again.

Very well, Sinclair thought. "We're no match for his cannons," he said simply. "Half the men will be dead before we reach his ship."

"We have a duty to our governor, Mr. Sinclair. A duty to the fine people of Virginia."

"Yes, sir. But —"

"What if he were to slip off during the fight? Teach knows these parts better than he knows his witch of a mother. I shall not be branded the man who let Blackbeard escape." Maynard dismissed him with a scowl, then looked about the others. "Two ships and sixty rifles up close will overwhelm whatever forces he has in the light of day. He's not going anywhere until then, mates, rest assured." He smiled at the last, nodded as if to encourage them. "Just bottle up the inlet." He then stepped away to his own quarters.

The local helmsmen gave Sinclair a knowing look as the men shuffled away to their various tasks, preparing to anchor just within Beaufort Inlet, and directions were shouted to the *Ranger*.

Sinclair gathered, again, with Williams at the charts. "At least we shall have the *tide* behind our efforts tomorrow," he said coldly.

"There is that," Williams laughed. Then, the two men got to work.

☠ ☠ ☠

The two sloops entered the narrow inlet at dawn. The *Ranger*, commanded by Hyde, took the lead with thirty-five armed men. The *Jane* carried Lieutenant Maynard, Sinclair, and another twenty. Maynard had ordered the King's colors hoisted on both to make their intentions undeniable while a smaller launch rowed just ahead to take depth soundings in the shallow water.

Through his telescope, Sinclair watched the small pirate crew scramble in response across their decks as the ship's anchor cable was cut and several cannons were rolled out into the early morning light. So much for any advantage of surprise. Though, he'd counted only ten men aboard as Blackbeard's ship, the *Adventure*, quickly retreated deeper into the channel. Perhaps they'd caught Teach with a reduced crew.

"He's on the run now," Maynard said smugly.

The pilot shook his head. "Nothing but submerged sandbanks up there, lieutenant. Best wait him out."

"Their loading the cannons, sir," Sinclair reported, watching Teach's men.

"The tide is with us." Maynard turned and hailed the *Ranger*. "Forward!" Maynard waved them ahead.

"But, even with the tide —"

Several cannons suddenly fired off the *Adventure* and the shots landed in sizable splashes mere feet away from the leading rowboat. Before the smoke had lifted from the *Adventure's* side, the small crew had already turned back.

Both sloops were bottoming out now, the sand beneath them tugging at the stunted keels. The wind was almost lifeless and slightly against them, no help in pushing the ships over the shallow water. Maynard ordered the oars out, as the men now set to using their backs to press forward. One sailor shouted back depths from the bowsprit while the men grunted and huffed against the strain of the oars. Each foot was gained with muscle and sweat, the two sloops creeping slowly ever forward towards the *Adventure*.

A large figure had now appeared at the stern of the pirate ship. And even without his telescope, Sinclair knew who it was.

Dressed in black, the man stood several inches taller than the other crew members, and his enormous beard hung like a living thing from his face. Blackbeard. Even trapped, outnumbered and surprised, he still looked imposing and startling.

The *Jane's* crew continued to struggle at the oars, dragging the ship inch by inch. Still too far for a volley of any merit, but close enough to hear the pirate when he began shouting out at them. "Damn you, villains!" The sturdy voice hollered over the reed-dotted gap between them, "Who are you?"

The voice was not that of the monster Sinclair expected, not the in-human thing that had haunted his dreams the past few weeks. It was merely the voice of a man. A bold man named Edward Teach who'd fought for the British Navy in the Queen Anne's Wars against Spain and distinguished himself as a sailor and marksman. An educated man who'd traveled the world several times over, amassed a fortune, and organized a crew of more than three hundred men and a half dozen vessels in less than two years. A man who lived free and made his own way and wore burning wicks in his beard just to intimidate people.

Maynard had stiffened at Blackbeard's voice, glanced briefly at Sinclair, then fixed his jacket straight before looking back towards the pirate. His mouth had opened only partly, as if to speak, when the voice boomed again.

"Cowardly puppy!" Teach yelled between his cupped hands. "From whence came ye, foul bandits!"

The Lieutenant's face reddened as he waved for the ship's speaking cone. "We sail under the colors of the King!" he called through the funnel, then added almost angrily, "We are no pirates!"

Teach seemed to smile at this last outburst, and Sinclair watched the pirate captain say something to several of his men, who laughed. They unex-pectedly looked no differently than any group of working men gathered at a

tavern table and likely had been the night before! Sinclair fought a grudging smile. Teach was cornered and outnumbered by almost forty men, and yet, still, able to remain confident and surly. He appeared a man completely in control of himself and the world around him.

Sinclair double-checked the musket pistol at his hip.

Shortly, Teach put his hand to his mouth again. "Why don't ye row o'er and properly introduce yourself aboard me ship!"

Maynard merely stood there for a moment as the men continued to struggle at the oars. "We will come aboard as soon as able, sir!" he said at last. "And with two sloops no less! Surrender now!"

Across the way, Teach produced a goblet and lofted it towards the two ships. "Then damnation seize my soul if I give ye quarters!" he shouted, drinking in mock toast. "Or take any from ye either!"

Amidst much shouting and effort, the *Ranger* suddenly freed itself and now floated freely in deeper tide water.

Sinclair watched through the scope as Teach turned and gave orders to his men. Hands moved to the sails.

"Setting sail, sir," Sinclair looked up at Maynard. Even as he spoke, the *Adventure's* foremast lifted against the faint wind.

"He's cornered," Maynard concluded. "There's nowhere to run."

Sinclair wished he were as confident. It was Blackbeard's cave they'd crawled into. Once the pirate got moving about in it, there was no telling what he might pull off.

The pirate's *Adventure* spun slowly about in the wind, more sails lifting, the small crew scurrying along the gangways and ratlines. He counted a dozen now, and the ship pushed forward, moving unhurriedly towards the sloops.

Crew members scurried to the gangways to fire at the vessel when it got closer. But then the pirate vessel suddenly veered starboard, making a run for a wide turn in the inlet. The *Ranger* pulled forward too, the rowers pulling even harder than before, some twenty guns closing in on Blackbeard and his men as more sailors now lined the ship's railing.

While Maynard watched the scene from the safety of his own quarter-deck, Sinclair ran to a free oar, settling in to row. "Heave, men!" he shouted. "Lay on those oars!"

Suddenly, the *Ranger* shuddered, and its crew stumbled to the railings and lines to hold themselves up. The vessel spun, healed port side, then froze half tilted in the water. The oarsman pulled to no avail.

A submerged sandbar! Sinclair swore, running to the railing. Teach, who knew his own inlet well, had set a trap for them and the *Ranger* had raced right into it.

The *Adventure* swung about then, closed in on the stranded *Ranger* like a wolf closing on a trapped lamb.

Sinclair counted ten cannons. Muskets fired intermittently at the pirate's ship as it pulled alongside. The reports of those guns sounded hollow in the quiet cove.

Then, however, the broadside fired from the *Adventure* as one single shot, disciplined and practiced, and the thunderous blast of ten cannons ripped apart the morning with a terrible din, flames spewing like dragon's breath between the two ships. Smoke lifted over her railings and briefly covered the pirate ship in a cloud of black mist. Cursing and screams now filled the inlet.

Sinclair slowly brought the telescope to his eye and looked over the damage to the *Ranger*. It was worse than even he'd feared. At least twenty men were down and their bodies lay strewn in awkward piles across its frenzied decks. Some were sprawled across the lines and blocks, as others slowly dragged themselves from the bloody carnage to the safety of the lowers. He found Hyde, the ship's acting captain, among those who weren't moving at all. The pirate's cannons had clearly been loaded with swan shot or nails and pieces of old iron. The men had been torn to shreds. He moved beyond the butchery to observe the *Adventure*.

Surprisingly, the pirate ship was also now slightly healed over. Its few manned oars slapped futilely at the still water. Dark bodies moved across the gangway, dropping and lifting various sails, working to free the ship from its apparent grounding. The broadside must have pushed her onto another sandbar, Sinclair sneered. Teach was now just as stuck as they!

The crew of the *Jane* redoubled their efforts to free the ship. All hands now tugged at the oars, slowly dragging her over the sand. Finally, with a roar from the crew, the ship broke free and coasted into deeper waters. Sinclair saw that the *Adventure* had also freed herself and was moving in for another kill.

"Make ready!" Maynard shouted suddenly, drawing his own pistol. "Fire at will!" Several muskets burst out in response.

"Sir!" Sinclair sprang to the quarterdeck. Maynard's eyes blazed narrow and piercing. "She's still too far for muskets."

"The cannons," Maynard blinked. "They'll —"

"They'll need more time to reload. She's undermanned and most of the men were working to get her unstuck. We should drive right into her."

Maynard's eyes widened now, glaring at the approaching pirate ship. Sporadic shots fired from the *Ranger* as it passed. Sinclair noticed the Lieutenant had moved away from the helm as the pilot and others waited for his word.

"You'll be killed," Maynard said, turning. He looked as if he smelled something foul. "We'll all be killed." He pushed past Maynard and made for the hatchway of the lower decks. Several men from the maindeck followed.

"What's 'e doing?" Williams asked.

Sinclair cursed. Then, he moved to the helm. "Run straight at 'em," he told the pilot. "Williams, take another five men below." Six had already fled with Maynard. "Something may come of this yet. Blackbeard would never believe we brought this many men and not one damn cannon. When we board, or get boarded, God help us, bring up the others. However necessary. We might have a surprise for him yet."

"Aye, Highlander." Williams winked, then moved for the hatchway himself, calling out names as he went. The ship was half cleared in moments, a half dozen bodies still running about its gangplanks. The *Adventure* loomed closer.

"Now," Sinclair shouted. "Mark to fire." Ten muskets and pistols lifted into the air. The two vessels pulled within feet of each other, running even along the starboard side. Priming pans clicked. Sinclair brought up his own pistol, couldn't find Teach and squared one of the other pirates in his sight. "Fire!"

The pistol jerked in Sinclair's hand, the spark lifting through the smoke as a dozen guns crackled in unison, the brief volley knocking back two bare-chested men from the *Adventure's* railing. Musket fire barked back from the pirate ship, and he crouched down, a short prayer caught halfway between his lips as black smoke lifted between the two ships and the report of gunfire continued. Someone spilled dead at Sinclair's feet.

Suddenly, a crude grenade sprang through the rising acrid smoke to explode on the *Jane's* decks. Sinclair lunged backwards as glass and iron scraps burst across the ship. The stench of black powder filled his nose. The back of his neck felt hot and sticky, as if he'd been cut, and the deck became a confusion of shouts and small detonations. Sinclair freed his cutlass and ran towards the railings for the impending boarding. The screaming grew more horrible, a dozen men carved by the makeshift shrapnel. Amidst the smoke, the deck had already grown slick with their blood.

The pirates leapt en masse across both railings with ease, swords and pistols drawn. There were only a dozen, but their shouts were excited and confident as they cut through the first men and then pressed deeper onto the *Jane*. Shots rang out again between the two groups.

Amid the smoke and yelling, Sinclair met one of Teach's men beneath the mizzenmast. The dark-skinned sailor snarled and slashed down at Sinclair with fury, but Sinclair blocked the stroke without difficulty, and passed to the left with his own. The pirate fell back briefly, his shoulder stabbed through, then charged again.

Their swords crashed for a second time, and fire shot up Sinclair's wrist, the pain of the blow running up his entire arm as he moved the blade again to deflect an ensuing swipe. Around them, bodies and movement crowded at every corner and a clanging sound more reminiscent of dozens of soup ladles and pans being clinked together, more so than any childhood fantasy of knights, now filled the decks. His own cutlass rang out like a broken goat's bell as the two blades met a final time.

Sinclair slid the blade down so that the two hilts caught together between them, then added his second hand to drive both hilts directly up into the pirate's startled face. There was a crunch of bone and the man fell back. The rest was easy. After, Sinclair looked over the rest of the battle.

Williams had sprung from the lower decks with the others, and it appeared as if Maynard and his gang had followed. The pirates were suddenly outnumbered two to one. Sinclair watched as Blackbeard, himself, used his free arm to lift one of his own men up from the deck. The two now fought side by side as the Virginia marines moved in. Surrounded, the massive pirate took several cuts as men fell away from his own cutting blows. Throughout, Blackbeard shouted curses at his foes and even laughed at the chaos surrounding them all. There were no apologies, Sinclair realized. Blackbeard did not hide behind manners or status. He was simply Blackbeard.

Several of his men had rallied to his side. Two other pirates, meanwhile, had jumped to the quarterdeck just behind Sinclair and wounded several men. Sinclair raced to meet them, and a handful of marines fell in beside him. The cutlasses swung to life again. The one pirate leapt to the ratlines, swinging over the men and landing safely in the frantic crowd below. Guns cracked again within the fray as the remaining pirate squared off against three men and the blades rattled to life once more.

Sinclair hurdled onto the stack of extra spars after the one who'd escaped, half-looking for Blackbeard himself. He found the man exactly where he expected to, at the center of the storm.

Blackbeard's body was now covered in bloody blotches, uneven crimson flowers that blossomed from dark centers. Sinclair could see that he'd been cut and stabbed. There must have been more than a dozen wounds. Still, Blackbeard pressed forward. Two more men fell before his blade, wounded and screaming. The others, some fifteen men, squeezed in on him, the few remaining pirates still fighting in a frame around the brutal scene.

Maynard himself stepped forward then and Blackbeard welcomed his sudden appearance with something that, to Sinclair, almost looked like a smile. The pirate lifted his dark-stained cutlass above his head and charged over the squirming bodies beneath to get to the Lieutenant.

Just feet away, Maynard lifted his gun and fired. The report and smoke split the space between them and Blackbeard staggered back with a mere grunt, a new dark hole appearing in his chest. But he staggered for only an instant, then moved in amid a flow of profanity.

A mere moment from Death, the Lieutenant clumsily freed the silver-wrought cutlass from his scabbard. It gleamed in the mid-morning sun briefly, then came up just enough to deflect the pirate's furious blow. With a hollow clang, the Lieutenant's sword snapped off at the hilt and Maynard fell back from the blow.

Blackbeard lifted his own cutlass again and stepped forward to finish him off.

Sinclair was waiting for him.

He'd stepped between the two men, Maynard scrambling back to his feet behind him, Blackbeard dripping and dark, his long unruly hair hanging in his eyes free and wild like lush ivy over some ancient statue. Sinclair swung his blade.

The pirate dipped beneath the swipe and lunged forward with his own stabbing thrust. Sinclair's blade snapped down on top of the cutlass, forcing Blackbeard's sword down. The pirate instantly swung hard with his other hand and Sinclair turned his head just in time to roll with most of the savage punch. What little of the blow had connected left him wobbly and cold. Anything more might have killed him outright.

Sinclair cut down again with his blade blocking Blackbeard's next attack. The swords jingled and prattled as the two stood boot to boot exchanging blows. Sinclair now recognized how much the many wounds had taken their toll. Blackbeard's breathing had grown more hoarse, his parries slower each time. Blackbeard was getting tired. He was dying.

Sinclair feigned another low thrust, then swung up and to the right, finally catching his opponent off guard. The blade cut across Blackbeard's throat and the large man stumbled backwards, bringing his free hand to the gory cut.

The other men moved in to finish the job or to take him prisoner. Sinclair knew Blackbeard was worth more captured. He imagined the man would spend months in jail, and then be paraded in a senseless trial by the Virginian governor for sake of the papers, only to be hanged before some pitiable horde of curious Virginians undoubtedly. Men and women who'd never been to sea, who'd never known risk or adventure themselves. Men and women who only knew fear.

"A fine sword ye be," the pirate grunted in a deep voice as the blood ran through his fingers. He coughed, then hocked red-tinged spit onto the deck beside him. "Who are ye, man?" he asked

"Sinclair, sir."

Blackbeard nodded, half smiled. His eyes looked distant and calm.

Sinclair's blade swung out a final time.

☠ ☠ ☠

"And I want the head hung from the bowsprit."

"Is that really necessary, sir?" Sinclair stood over Blackbeard's body with a sheet of old canvas as the rest of the crew tended to the wounded, finished securing the few prisoners, and commandeered the *Adventure*.

"Do you disagree, Mr. Sinclair?" Maynard glared. "I'm half-inclined to believe you almost admired this thing."

Sinclair answered honestly. "I suppose that's partly true."

"Praise his death, Sinclair. He was a filthy pirate and every pirate deserves death."

Sinclair shook his head. "That's just the thing, Maynard," he said, thinking of all the men who'd brought them to this point. "We're all filthy pirates, in our way." He finished laying the rotted canvas over the still body. "Teach was just the only one with the heart to admit it."

Maynard's eyes hardened as he glared at Sinclair. His hands were now clasped behind his back, his chin out.

"Mr. Sinclair, I will personally present my full report to Captain Brand upon our arrival. Of our hard-fought victory and my scheme of hiding our true numbers below deck. And, as your commanding officer, I shall expect your full concurrence with my given statement." Maynard's eyes burned fiercely now, cornered and angry. "Is that understood?"

Sinclair stared back, his own eyes likely betraying his true emotions. He thought of everything he'd seen in the last two weeks. Of his promising career and Maynard's influence therein. He thought of the sun hanging now just above the *Jane's* masts and imagined the next dawn. And, he thought of Genny and the boys.

"Yes, sir," he found himself saying, and, then, tried it again to see if familiarity made it come any easier. "Yes, sir."

It had not.

NOTES: *Lieutenant Maynard soon became forever known as the man who killed Blackbeard, the last true scourge of the seven seas, in hand-to-hand combat. Maynard ordered the pirate's severed head hung as a trophy from the bowsprit of his ship and returned to Virginia, where he collected commendations and reward money. In all, Blackbeard had received five pistol shots and twenty severe sword wounds before finally falling, and one common tale adds that even his headless corpse swam defiantly around the sloop three times before sinking! After interrogating the surviving pirates, Maynard and his men later discovered much of Blackbeard's treasure hidden in the barn of one Tobias Knight, Governor Eden's (of North Carolina) secretary. Meanwhile, the political problems of Governor Spotswood (of Virginia) were shortly forgotten, as planned, and he entered private life shortly thereafter with 80,000 acres and three successful iron furnaces.*

Though Blackbeard was notorious for his cruelty, there is no record of his men ever once harming those who surrendered without a fight, and he was later known for being particularly respectful towards women prisoners. While his death was not the end of piracy along the Atlantic Coast, it certainly heralded the end of the "Golden Age" of piracy as the colonies became increasingly organized and committed to ending the high-sea threat once and for all.